Preface

In 1938, the name Christian Bugge was o........ .... lips. She was a sturdy rescue vessel with a courageous crew, dedicated to saving lives in the North Sea. Forty three years later I saw her in the Seychelles. She was rotten from neglect and riddled with toredo worm, yet still reluctant to give in to old age and settle on the bottom of Victoria Harbour.

Two families came under the spell of this famous ship. We dedicated a part of our lives to the restoration of the Christian Bugge and after two and a half years were rewarded with an eleven month adventure which held both elation and despair. We marvelled at remote islands in the Indian Ocean and quaked under gunfire in the Caribbean. We experienced the solitude of a starry sky above a tranquil ocean and the intoxication of a raging storm.

Throughout the voyage, the three children had to continue their education with the Christian Bugge rule of 'school at sea - holiday in port'! The curriculum was extended to incorporate practical sessions in sailing, navigation and survival. They learnt to identify clouds, fish, islands, birds, and other vessels .

Our destination was Plymouth, England. Many moments of near disaster made me feel that we would never make it.

However, here we all are........

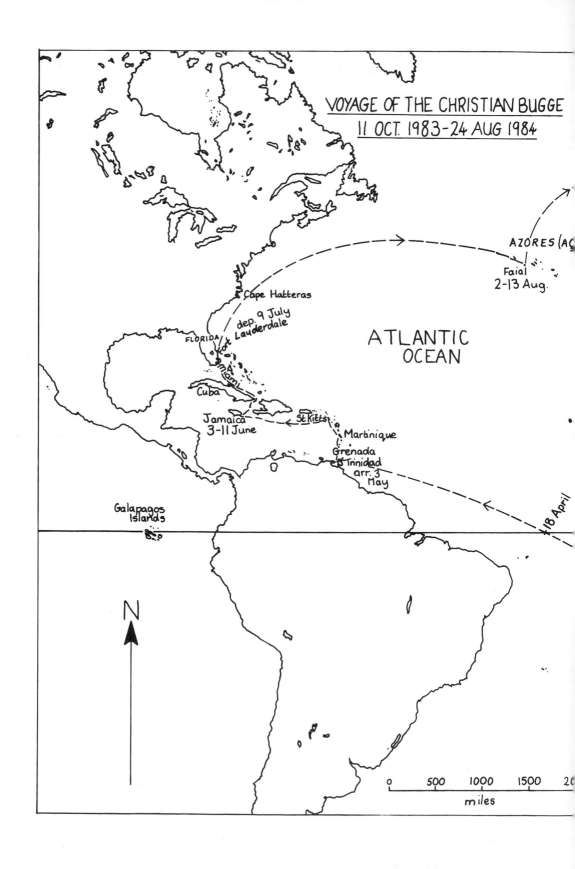

VOYAGE OF THE CHRISTIAN BUGGE
11 OCT. 1983 – 24 AUG 1984

AZORES (AÇ

Faial
2-13 Aug.

Cape Hatteras

dep. 9 July
Fort Lauderdale

FLORIDA

ATLANTIC
OCEAN

Miami

Cuba

Jamaica
3-11 June

St Kitts

Martinique

Grenada
Trinidad
arr. 3
May

Galapagos
Islands

18 April

N

0   500   1000   1500   20
miles

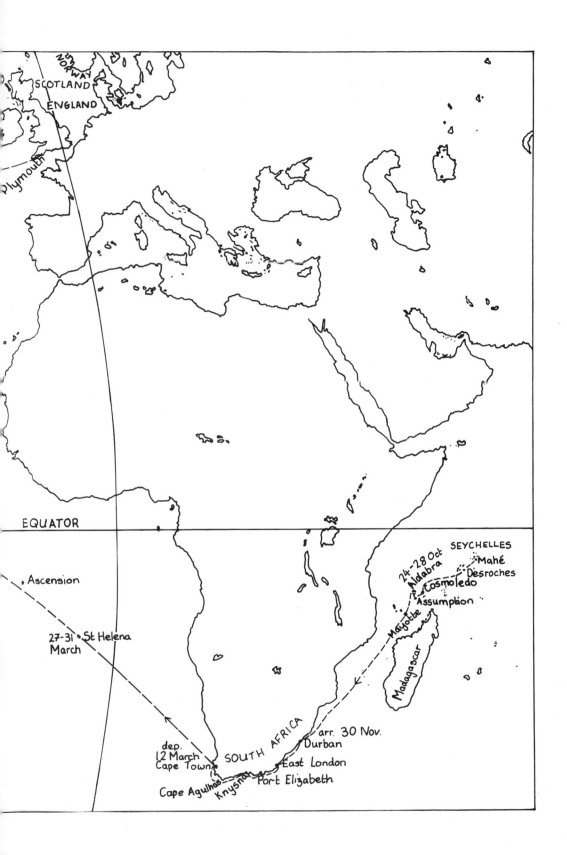

NORWAY

SCOTLAND

ENGLAND

Plymouth

EQUATOR

SEYCHELLES

24-28 Oct
Aldabra   Mahé
      Cosmoledo   Desroches
   Assumption

Ascension

Mayotte

27-31 • St Helena
March

Madagascar

arr. 30 Nov.
Durban

dep.
12 March   SOUTH AFRICA
Cape Town   East London
         Cape Agulhas Knysna Port Elizabeth

First published 1988 by Andrew and Helen Smallwood
39 St. Ambrose Close, Dinas Powys, South Glamorgan.

Copyright © Helen Smallwood 1988

Printed and bound by Colorcraft Ltd. Hong Kong.
Cover by Zee Graphic Design
Cover illustration by Andrew James

Acknowledgements

If it weren't for the enthusiasm of my family and friends, this book would still be on loose sheets in a cluttered cupboard.

Thanks to Andy's philosophy that most things can be achieved with patience and determination, I made friends with the computer and acquired a working knowledge of printing jargon. His logical approach scaled all the problems down to a manageable size. He illustrated the star constellations at the start of each chapter and generally stopped me panicking over deadlines. Lucy kindly compacted homework and leisure activities in order to draw all the maps. Andy's brother Robin turned editor and typesetter overnight with apparent pleasure. My thanks to them and the rest of the family who offered advice and encouragement.

I am grateful to Pat, John and Joan Hook for being part of our adventure and to Martin Shaw for his colourful contribution to the story, also for some photographs.

Peter Hingston, Author of 'The *Greatest* Little Business Book', gave me sound, practical, publishing advice and his warmest wishes for success.

Protea Colour Prints Ltd. kindly gave me permission to reproduce aeria photographs of Knysna and Cape Town.

Helen Smallwood

Contents

1. Tropical Setting   7

2. A Noble Past   13

3. Many A Slip   19

4. A Change Of Plan   27

5. Departure At Last   37

6. Hazardous Beginning via The Amirantes   41

7. From Baguettes To Biltong   53

8. Gales and City Glitter   61

9. Unscheduled Operation   68

10. Knysna   74

11. Cape of Storms   84

12. An Island on its Own   92

13. The Christian Bugge Academy   97

14. What Happened to the Rice?   105

15. Savouring the East Caribbean   112

16. "I May Need Some Assistance"   120

17. American Pie   130

18. Water and Wine   137

19. Topsail Finish   151

Afterword   156

PASSAGE FROM PARADISE

BY

HELEN SMALLWOOD

Tropical Setting

For me it was first and foremost an adventure. It was a way of cutting loose from hum drum routine and the pressures of modern civilisation. That adventure lingers in memories which are vivid enough to brighten a drab day.

* * * * *

It all began on the 9th May 1981, at a Shakespearian party, on the island of Mahé in the Seychelles. As Cleopatra I made a grand entrance, flashing dark eyes and golden costume, but my ego was quickly deflated when I realised I stood among four other expatriate Cleopatras! As I stared bemused at a 6 foot 6 inch hairy Titania and listened to Lady Macbeth complaining about the shortage of flour on the island and problems of whipping cream in the tropical heat, my Marc Anthony slid away to talk to Cassius about a Norwegian Lifeboat lying in Victoria Harbour. This vessel, the Christian Bugge, was to change the lives of two families dramatically over the next three years.

* * * * *

But how did we come to be on an island in the Indian Ocean?

In 1979, Andy, my husband had given up a comfortable job with the Civil Service in Taunton, Somerset for a British aided post with the Seychelles government. At that time, anything was preferable to working on designs for roads which did not have much chance of being built, so I encouraged the move and looked forward to living five degrees South of the equator on Mahé, the main island in the Seychelles group. Our son Iain was then almost ten and Lucy six. Naturally they were to come with us, since none of us liked the idea of boarding schools, and anyway we had heard that there was an International School in Victoria, the capital town, incidentally the smallest capital in the world. It was hard to imagine what it would be like living on a lump of land, only seventeen miles by five miles at its widest point, with all that water around it. I remember looking at the tiny dots representing the Seychelles on the globe and sensing the loneliness of the islands before I ever saw them.

That loneliness proved to be exquisite. The skirts of the granitic mountains conceal lush valleys and sunbirds, quiet coves and lazy people. The long curving white strand of Beauvallon with its splendid Takamaka trees standing sentinel to its treasure, is an unforgettable picture in my mind. Luxuriating in the warm waters of that azure bay, I could look towards the ancient mountains that command the centre of the island. Strange to think they have been there for several hundred million years but man has only lived there for two hundred years or so. The first recorded landing was in 1609 by three ships of the British East India Company, but it was not until 1770 that the first attempt at colonisation was made by an expedition of settlers from Mauritius. In 1814 they were ceded to the British at the Treaty of Paris and from then on were administered as dependency of Mauritius. They were given Crown Colony status in 1903 and gained independence in 1976.

As a family we settled easily into the community. The transient Europeans were easy-going people, used to working away from their homeland. They were welcoming and ever hospitable, but with a protective shield at the ready in case anyone got to close to them. I put this down to two things - the colonial stiff upper lip attitude and the fact that expatriates are never in one place long enough to form deep friendships. If they let it happen, then their tower begins to crumble.

We had some good times - dinner parties, amateur dramatics, Scottish dancing - the kinds of things one does when there's no television. I even absolved myself of the guilt at being in paradise by taking a teaching job at the International School. At least I felt I earned my time on the beach and it gave me a cast iron excuse for not going to those coffee mornings and bridge parties. Besides, I was happier talking to five year olds than to the ladies of the Corona Society which seemed to me to be a sort of Women's Institute for nomads.

We spent our first few weeks in a house near the top of La Misère mountain where our shoes turned a lovely shade of green with the damp, and where we first heard the fruit bats. They would wheel over the house at dusk, and as night fell, would create a dreadful screeching and squawking racket as they bickered over the best paw paws, jackfruits or bananas.

We moved to a house further down the hill where it wasn't so damp, and where we had a superb view of the approaches to Victoria Harbour, some of the offshore islands, and the coast road meandering from Victoria to the airport. Here we got to know our landlord Philippe Lalanne and his gentle wife Lise, both of french extraction. They lived in a small house close by and I have never met a more generous couple. Philippe, a wiry stick of a man with white hair and twinkling eyes, had a myriad of tales to tell about his years in East Africa for the British Colonial administration, followed by his service with the Seychelles Ministry of Agriculture. He was a man of the land, an authority on birds and other wild life in the islands - a character to be reckoned with. I see him most vividly with a cigarette hanging from the corner of his mouth, leading the goats out to graze - scolding them roughly when they stepped out of line. If one of them became sick or was about to give birth he would stay with it for hours, finally returning to his favourite chair on the veranda where Lise would instantly produce a cup of tea. Sitting here, looking out across the sea he would amuse himself by feeding rice to the birds on

Lise and Lucy enjoying late afternoon sun together in the garden.

the little table at his elbow. I don't know how old he was - certainly venerable enough to tease the religious and political leaders of the country when he felt inclined.

Lise was a quieter character, treasured friend and confidant to my daughter Lucy. I remember Lucy sneaking out of the house at first light, via the window because she couldn't reach the bolts on the door. Lise would always be up by 5.45a.m., making tea or tending her plants. She and Lucy used to talk and laugh together until the rest of us were up and about. Sometimes Lise would sew pretty clothes for Lucy, or help her do some needlework herself. When we finally left Mahé, both of us were deeply affected at parting from such a thoughtful person.

Iain and Lucy did well at the International School where small classes facilitated individual teaching, but although they mixed with children from eighteen other countries, they got to know few of the Seychellois children because it was the policy of the socialist government for them to be educated only in the local schools. This tended to set us Europeans apart as a privileged group, which saddened me. It was not impossible for British parents to get their children into a local school under the free system of education. However, this did present a language problem, particularly for older children who took time to learn the Seychelles creole, a kind of mutilated ancient french, recently gaining recognition as a written language within the islands.

The Seychellois people are a mixture of African, Oriental and European races, their wide range of skin colour defying the terms black and white. When we first arrived, it was impressed upon me by a fellow Britisher that these people were generally sour and unhelpful. I found them shy and uncommunicative at first meeting but warm and friendly as they got to know you. They are gentle, insular people, concerned with finding the easiest path through life - mildly excited by petty squabbles over status and jobs. Visitors to the Tropics usually dress sloppily in baggy shorts, T-shirts and the like. They are shamed by the Seychellois who dress beautifully on most occasions. A Seychellois girl would not dream of wearing anything but a dress and proper shoes to go shopping in town. Her man would wear long trousers and a tidy shirt unless relaxing at home or on the beach. They might both be slightly disapproving of the topless tourists who littered Beauvallon beach. Prior to one of the local public holidays, I saw a notice in a hotel lobby requesting guests to wear their bikini tops, so as not to offend the Seychellois people in their leisure time.

Pat and John Hook arrived in the Seychelles six months after us. John was sent out on British Aid as Chief Forester whilst Pat became a colleague of mine at the International School. They had spent some time in Jamaica during the Seventies and had adopted a Jamaican girl called Joan. Joan had been abandoned as a tiny baby by her real mother and had become an unhappy toddler in an orphanage. Pat and John were looking for a daughter at this time but were advised not to take Joan because she was reputed to be 'difficult'. They ignored advice, adopted Joan and took her back to Britain. For many months she ate little and spoke hardly at all while her new guardians coaxed and comforted with infinite patience. By the time I met her she was a robust seven year old with a loud voice and a big appetite!

I liked the island life dominated by a fierce sun and friendly ocean. The children swam, canoed, sailed dinghies or windsurfed. When darkness fell, always at 6.30p.m., they read or entertained themselves with old fashioned pursuits. Few of the world's problems encroached upon our existence and I made the most of it, knowing that we would have to face them again some day. Of course Seychelles had its own internal difficulties. In 1977 Albert René, then Prime Minister, had snatched power from James Mancham in an almost bloodless coup and pronounced it Revolution. From then on he was in the unenviable position of having to look over his shoulder, particularly towards U.K. where Mancham took refuge along with other prominent figures. Much of René's social reform was good. It improved the quality of life for a great many people, but for others, the extreme Communist ideals were hard to swallow. Only two months after our arrival, hundreds of school children took to the streets to march in protest at René's plans to make National Youth Service compulsory. Cars were overturned, buses set on fire, and the Revolution's giant statue of Zomme Libre (free man) festooned with toilet paper. It was probably the nearest that Victoria will ever come to a riot. People were imprisoned, the schools were closed for a week, and when everything had simmered down, plans for the National Youth Service went ahead as before. At the age of fifteen, young people were to continue their education at one of the NYS camps where they would receive paramilitary training. It was not compulsory to serve the prescribed two years but it was immediately understood that it would be extremely difficult to obtain a job or continue with further education if this training were rejected. Later, the seven of us were to depend heavily upon the NYS because Pat obtained a full time job teaching English there!

Early in 1981 the mad idea of sailing back to the U.K. had occurred to Andy and I when we saw a thirty six foot schooner rigged yacht called Petit Prince, up for sale by auction. She had been on her way from Tahiti to France when the crew was forced to abandon her in Victoria because the owner had gone bankrupt. The crew was repatriated and Petit Prince fell into disrepair. The bids rose too high for us and a crazy American, nicknamed Scottie, sporting a girl on each arm, became the new owner. He spent months patching the hull in haphazard fashion, then disappeared one night along with an inflatable dinghy and other valuable items from the boatyard. He had never sailed before the auction, but I believe he managed to scrounge a few tips from yacht club members before he left.

By May we had to start making plans to leave Seychelles by normal methods, as the end of Andy's two year contract loomed near. We contemplated various air routes home and I gave in my notice at school.

It was Ron Jurd, marine consultant and very good friend, who put the spanner in the works. Casually, he mentioned to John and Andy that an old Norwegian Rescue Ship, Colin Archer design, was rotting in the harbour and might be coming up for sale.

Andy's first glimpse of Christian Bugge.

This little snippet of information gradually sank in. Andy and I talked when we were alone and pondered the idea of a partnership, knowing that John also yearned for a long ocean passage. It seemed that John had also taken the bait, with the result that broaching the subject at the Shakespearian party was easy, and an expedition to look over the boat was arranged. I freely admitted that my imagination had been fired even before I saw Christian Bugge. I was also anxious to press on with the deal because it was rumoured that a Scotsman was interested in buying her as a 'drinking vessel'!

Andy and John came back from their first visit with a gleam in their eyes and I knew then that I would get my adventure. Within the week we had placed a deposit of 6,000 Rupees, I had withdrawn my resignation at school, and Andy had obtained reasonable assurance that he could extend his contract. This was all before I had even seen the boat!

On my first expedition to look over Christian Bugge I dislodged giant palm spiders from the rigging and gazed in horror at the layers of oily grime and dead cockroaches - not to mention the live ones - below decks. Yet I was impressed by the massive oak frames and the solid feel of her. I agreed with John when he said, "She has good vibes". However, after ten months of neglect she was leaking badly. Even with constant pumping she sat low in the water, particularly at the stern.

The old galley was not a pretty sight.

The old name plate convinced us that we were looking at a famous Colin Archer Rescue Ship.

A Noble Past

On the 22nd May 1981, the Smallwoods and the Hooks became joint owners of the Christian Bugge for the nominal sum of 30,000 Rupees (approximately £3,000) which was paid to Lindblad's Travel Agency. We enlisted the help of a motor cruiser to tow her to the inner harbour.

At this stage we knew very little about her, only that she was an ex-Norwegian Rescue Ship, built in 1935 and had been sailed to the Seychelles in 1967. The rest of her history filtered through little by little with the help of John Leather's book, 'Colin Archer and the seaworthy double ender', The Norwegian Rescue Service, The Colin Archer Society, and a Norwegian couple living in the Seychelles at the time. Mr and Mrs Aasebo were overjoyed to hear that we intended to restore the Christian Bugge and sail her back to Europe. Like many Norwegians, they had grown up with stories of her daring rescues as she patrolled the Norwegian coastline between 1935 and 1967. Mr Aasebo said that all Norwegians would be very happy to hear about our project. He also obtained information from the Norwegian Maritime Museum in Oslo which he translated into English and recorded on tape for us.

Christian Bugge was designed by Bjarne Aas and built by Knut Christensen and Company of Moen near Risor on the South coast of Norway. It was at a time when sail was giving way to power so that some of the early sailing rescue ships were being fitted with auxiliary engines. She was one of the first to be designed as a motor sailer, with an overall length of 56 feet 3 inches, beam 17 feet, and draught 9 feet 6 inches. Like all boats built in the Colin Archer tradition, she was heavily constructed to withstand rough seas. The frames were 6 inch by 5 inch sawn oak in pairs with 11 inch gaps and 2 inch oak planks fastened with trenails. In fact Christian Bugge had a particular reputation as a 'stormbird', proving herself time and time again in violent seas. These facts gave us some comfort when we thought of the voyage that lay ahead of us.

We were amused to note that Christian Bugge was the very first rescue ship

The Maritime Museum in Oslo supplied us with this photograph of a model of Christian Bugge

to have a loo installed! The Norwegian Rescue Service had existed for forty two years without such luxuries and there were still people at that time who felt that this kind of comfort was unnecessary!

At some time a ten foot high aluminium wheelhouse was added and the rig was reduced by decreasing the size of the main mast. In 1967 Lindblad Travel Agency bought her and fitted her out in Mombasa to act as the first charter boat in Seychelles. For twelve years she ferried passengers around the inner group of granitic islands and also through the Amirantes as far as Aldabra, 900 miles away. In 1979 the central area below decks had been completely lined with polystyrene and GRP as a fish hold, by a syndicate of local men who converted Christian Bugge for fishing and turtling.

So - we had bought a dilapidated boat with a worthy past. What next?

The four of us talked far into the night probing each other's minds to find out what we expected from the project and what resources we could draw on. We had allowed imagination and instinct to take over and now it was time to face up to practicalities. Fortunately we agreed on all major issues. All we needed was time and money. John was able to extend his contract for six months and Andy for one year, bringing both families to a finishing date early in November 1982. We had no way of telling whether seventeen months would be enough to complete the restoration and be ready to sail off into the blue, but we were not short of determination and optimism.

This was put to the test when our first major problem of how to get Christian Bugge out of the water, arose. It was a bad time because the large slipway cradles were in need of repair and new ones were about to be constructed.

Christian Bugge was taking in a lot of water. A simple sawdust bath known as 'fothering' bought us a little time. A large biscuit tin, peppered with holes and filled with sawdust, was towed round the outside of the hull below water. Miraculously, the leaky planking absorbed the sawdust and gave us considerably less pumping each day. It was only a temporary respite and would need redoing if there was any untoward movement of the boat or the sea around her.

A month went by. We used the time to strip her as bare as possible. Andy and John spent hours disconnecting the engine, uncoupling the propeller shaft and removing miscellaneous debris. They employed a boat boy called Jimmy who could turn his hand to anything and who was later to act as a very able link with Creole workmen. Jimmy used his wiry strength to loosen the heavy bolts of the wheelhouse. It was also his job to shin up aloft and disconnect the rigging, which he did as effortlessly as if the mast were a coconut palm.

We bought a dory with two outboard engines for 7,000 Rupees which we used as general workboat and ferry. Later, during the voyage, this sturdy craft was to become invaluable after calamity struck one windy night.

At last, towards the end of June, we obtained permission to use the Port crane with forty ton capacity, to lift her out of the water. Having removed masts, engine and deckhouse with a smaller crane, the tense moment arrived.

Some of our friends came to hold their breath with us.

Christian Bugge parts with her deck-house.

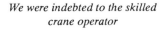

The crane took up position and cables and spreaders were prepared. Andy dived into the oily water to fix metal shoes under the keel. As Christian Bugge began to rise out of the sea it became clear that the cables were too long. Weight also seemed to be a problem because the back of the crane was lifting clear of the ground! We had to give up and try again the next day.

Again we timed the operation for high water. This time Andy doubled the cables and secured them with gigantic shackles. They were then on the short side, returning to the spreaders at a sharp angle from the bulwarks. An even bigger crowd of spectators hovered in the background. As the crane took Christian Bugge's full weight, we heard crunching noises of disintegrating bulwarks. She was lowered once more to have blocks of wood placed between the cables and the hull. Again the operator calmly began the lift. This time she rose smoothly and silently until she finally came to rest on solid ground and was supported by John's new props. We were relieved and full of admiration for the crane operator who ignored his alarm bell throughout the lift. We later calculated that Christian Bugge must have weighed forty eight tons!

Pat and I looked with awe at the massive hull that would one day have to take the seven of us across the oceans. The account of Christian Bugge's most famous rescue was running through my head..............

On Sunday 3rd April 1938, a violent storm struck the West coast of Norway. It was reported that the Rokta, a cargo vessel of 368 tons was aground on rocky shallows, having missed the lighthouse warning. Christian Bugge left Christiansund immediately and reached the area within a few hours.

From a distance of 500 metres the captain, John Bakken, and his crew could see only the aft section of Rokta lodged on the rocks. The front half had already disappeared into deep water. Through tremendous waves that were breaking right over the boat, the crew of Christian Bugge could see the Norwegian flag still flying and one man clinging to the deck of the wreck. In fact eleven men were still on board, all expecting death at any moment. John Bakken discussed the chances with his crew and radioed headquarters that the odds were 100:1 against success.

Despite the odds, Bakken and his crew went in closer waiting for the right waves to surf over the shallows. They tried to fire rescue lines to Rokta but these did not catch on the wreck and it soon became apparent that time was running out. The wreck began to slide. Christian Bugge moved in as close as she dared. The men on board Rokta leapt into the angry sea just as the remains of the wreck slipped beneath the waves. Christian Bugge picked up seven men, six of whom survived.

This real life drama was shared by many people all over Norway with the advent of short-wave radio. The crew of the Christian Bugge all received the King's award for bravery and Arnulf Overland wrote a poem called 'The Seamen of Hustadvika' honouring the heroic rescue, which is still quoted to this day.

Back to the present and some hard facts.

Close examination of the sodden timber revealed the expected worm damage to the planking, but ever optimistic, we told each other that she would be back in the water within five months. If we had known that we would have to more than double that figure, a note of despair might have crept in, but luckily, the project swept us on, anaesthetising us to all difficulties, including the slow realisation that 50% of the planks were to need replacing!

John's position as Chief Forester, equipped him admirably for the task of searching for timber. We needed a great deal of 'takamaka', the local hardwood favoured by Seychellois boatbuilders. No sawn timber stocks were held on the island, so it was necessary to go into the forest to select suitable trees. Kiln drying facilities were available, but much of the timber cut at the start of the project was able to be seasoned for a year or more. Some of the more unusual timbers needed for internal work, were only to be found deep in the forest, where they were felled and pit sawn on the spot, so that they could be carried out on the heads of the workers.

Andy spent several days taking the lines off the high and dry Christian Bugge so that he could design a rig that would take us comfortably and efficiently from A to B and would also follow the Colin Archer tradition of pure sailing vessel. We were still mulling over several alternatives when Andy and I took our home leave - six weeks of scouring Hong Kong and England for parts and ideas. We loaded our bags with books, chronometer, sextant, copper lamps, binoculars, tallow, wet weather gear and various items for amusing children on a long voyage. Andy's brother Robin gave us an assurance that he would act as our U.K. purchasing agent, a most welcome gift.

Our non-sailing relatives were naturally dubious about the project. In her anxiety, my mother did not expect to see us ever again and it was no use telling her that we had no intention of joining Neptune at this stage of our lives. Iain had outgrown the International School so we left him behind in England with very understanding friends, Wendy and Malcolm Watchman, where he attended a comprehensive school for a year, and where he benefited from a rural environment. He was only too pleased to be out of the way during the mucky stages of the renovation.

She remained on props for eleven months - five months longer than we anticipated

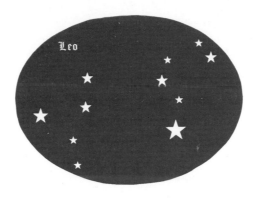

Many A Slip

Our shopping in Hong Kong had left us feeling that things were moving fast. On returning to the lazy swell of the Indian Ocean we realised that the pace was less urgent. John had had problems with caulkers and carpenters. He had had to look for replacements to do a more thorough job with the planking. We couldn't afford to skimp this part of the project. A forty seven year old hull needs expert care and attention to preserve its strength.

Ron Jurd, who has spent all his life with wooden boats, had become our 'guru' right from the start. He had tapped and jabbed his way from stem to stern, finally pronouncing that it could be a lot worse! On his advice we had elected to use the traditional types of caulking material. This meant importing large quantities of white lead from South Africa and finding a source of tallow in U.K. A considerable part of our leave was spent on the tallow hunt, until we accidentally discovered a supplier only a mile away from our home on the outskirts of Bristol! Ron Jurd explained the ideal mix of white lead, tallow, red lead powder and gold size. Jimmy, our English speaking 'Jack-of-all-trades', relayed instructions to caulkers and carpenters, while Andy and John kept an eagle eye open for careless workmanship.

The skippers' job at this time, four months after the purchase of Christian Bugge, was sand-blasting fuel tanks and other metalware. It was an earsplitting, exhausting task which made them drink gallons of water under the tropical sun. They also organised the removal of the four hundred pound winch from the foredeck, by crane, to make way for the bowsprit at a later date. We had at last decided on a sail plan. Christian Bugge would be a gaff rigged ketch, based on the early sailing rescue ships, with a mizzen about half the height of the main mast. This rig would include a topsail to give her more sail area than when she was first constructed.

John had the responsibility of finding a suitable piece of timber for a new stem. He took a trip to Curieuse, a small island off the coast of Praslin, 25 miles

Our best shipwright using the adze to shape the new stem.

The stem in place.

away, and studied the curves of the takamaka trees there. He found the shape he wanted and in due course the tree was felled and shipped back to Mahe, where our senior carpenter worked on the final shaping. By the end of November it was in position and looking good.

John did not always see eye to eye with the carpenters. One problem concerning two replacement planks that needed twist at the stern, became a minor incident on site. It is not the custom in Seychelles, to steam planks for shaping although they sometimes soak them. On this occasion the workmen resisted John's suggestions until finally, a compromise had to be found. Jimmy organised a 'boiler' in an open length of pipe welded at the ends to hold water. The planks were brewed and shaped successfully.

Progress was infinitely slower than we had hoped. We had bought Christian Bugge in May, hoping to have her back in the water by Christmas at the latest. This was not to be, and although it was disappointing, those of us who were closely involved with the work knew that a great deal had been accomplished. Interested bystanders were not quite so sure but they tried to give us encouragement.

One hiccup which we could not have foreseen, was the arrival in November of South African mercenaries on a Swazi aeroplane, to attempt a coup. Luckily for all of us, the plotters were discovered in the nick of time, just as they were leaving the airport with bags of toys containing arms in concealed compartments. Most of the mercenaries escaped on an Air India plane the same night, having held staff and passengers as terrified hostages, but a handful retreated into the hills. The

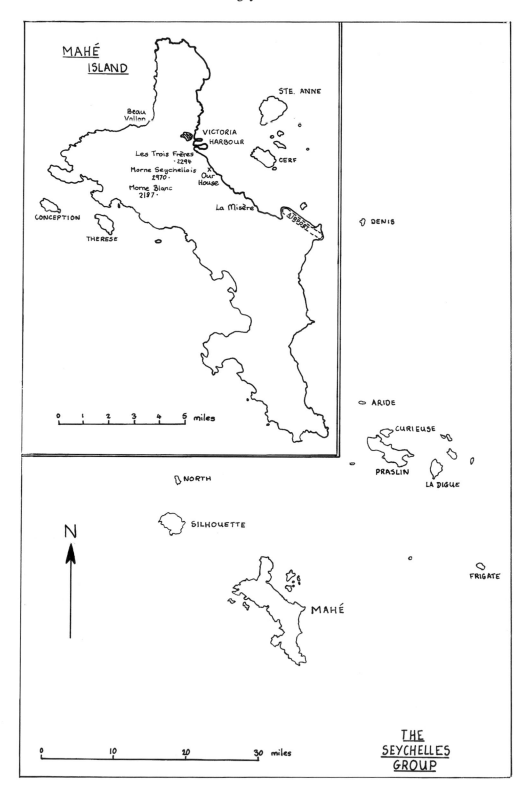

MAHÉ ISLAND

Beau Vallon

STE. ANNE

VICTORIA HARBOUR

Les Trois Frères
· 2294
Morne Seychellois
2970 ·
Morne Blanc
2187 ·

X Our House

CERF

La Misère

AIRPORT

CONCEPTION

THERESE

DENIS

0 1 2 3 4 5 miles

ARIDE

NORTH

CURIEUSE

PRASLIN

LA DIGUE

N

SILHOUETTE

FRIGATE

MAHÉ

0   10   20   30 miles

THE SEYCHELLES GROUP

seven hundred strong Seychelles Army stepped in with two left feet and fired mortar shells in the general direction of the airport, which certainly caused a great deal of damage and probably gave them some fun. Complete curfew was imposed for five days while the authorities rounded up the fleeing mercenaries.

Once the initial fright was over, most of us enjoyed the enforced confinement. It became a challenge to make a meal out of what was left in the cupboard, and we had all the time in the world to listen to music, play card games and even talk. Some expatriates started a telephone quiz. Others just drank their beer stocks. Andy spent the time working on a navigation program for his HP41C calculator.

Life gradually got back to normal but there was feeling of unease in Victoria. Army uniforms seemed to spring up everywhere and security at the damaged airport was stringent for a time. Andy and John were glad to get back to our neglected old lady.

One day our purchasing agent, Andy's brother Robin, happily informed us by telex that he had made a down payment on our behalf, for a reconditioned Gardner 5LW engine.

We marked Christmas by allowing ourselves one whole day off.

The New Year brought more than our fair share of frustrations in the form of delayed shipments and a sudden drying up of supplies of a resorcinol glue, which we had used in copious quantities. We hoarded our last tins in secret niches and tried not to be downhearted.

On the credit side, John and Andy began the initial shaping of the main mast with a portable chain saw mill. Silently, we thanked the Seychelles Electricity Corporation for providing us with a Norwegian pine telegraph pole!

Pat and I were called on for cleaning, scraping and painting when our teaching jobs and home commitments permitted. The children helped when they were in the mood, otherwise they played amongst boatyard scrap - much more fun than a white sand beach!

Robin was also beavering away on our behalf, scouring the Portsmouth and Southampton area for second-hand items wherever possible. Some specialised parts for the rigging posed more of a problem and had to be made to order.

At last there came a day when the humdrum activities were punctuated by the arrival of our first shipment containing engine, echo sounder, sea cocks, upholstery material, various chunky bolts and other metalware. Robin had done his job well. The boatyard gang clustered admiringly round the engine and oohed and aahed over the propeller and stern gear, anxious to make it ready for installation. At least it spurred us on.

We were also spurred on by a friend of ours, Alan Smith, a community policeman near Andy's home in Bristol. Having spent a month with us in Seychelles during 1980, doing the kinds of things advertised in holiday brochures, he decided he would like to spend another month with us making himself useful. I must admit that when he first put the idea to us, I thought he was crazy. He came in April, stepping off the Jumbo into the sticky heat of the calm period between the two monsoon seasons. He relaxed for an hour or two and then accompanied us to

Christian Bugge. Alan was not content to watch for long on that first day. He climbed down into the forepeak and started scraping old paintwork which had to be stripped off the deck beams. He was stoic, cheerful and busy, but careful to keep his red hair and freckly skin out of the sun. Strangely enough, he is grateful to us for giving him a wonderful holiday, but he gave us far more.

For a while there was rapid progress. Bilges were battened to take flexible water tanks, giving us a total capacity of 280 gallons. Copper sheets which had been removed from the waterline, were put back and cleaned with a sanding disc. The stainless steel propeller shaft was manoeuvred into position and the rudder post and yolk bolted into place with much sweat and strain. Sea cocks were fitted and tested. The winch was repaired, and new beds were welded to the existing frame in preparation for the engine.

We were all impatient to reach the cosmetic stage now, so as soon as caulking was completed and the work force occupied with plugging topsides, we plastered two coats of epoxy coal tar onto thirsty planks below waterline. Two coats of antifouling followed as rapidly as the excellent tropical drying conditions permitted. One particular painting session was hampered by a cloud of bees which decided to swarm on our scaffolding. The Seychellois workmen took great delight in scooping them up in their hands looking for the queen, but the rest of us gave them a wide berth.

We cautiously turned to the tide tables in search of possible dates for a crane lift. June 8th became our target and we worked relentlessly towards that special Tuesday, a culmination of eleven months toil.

The rudder in place with the new propeller.

Caulking and planking in progress.

Once the topsides were plugged and planed, the sanding, filling and painting began. After spending endless days filling the rough surface with a white lead mix between prime coats, we decided it was the kind of job that could go on for ever, so we stopped and contented ourselves with a rugged workboat finish befitting an old timer with a noble past.

As June 8th drew nearer, we longed for just a few more daylight hours each day. With only twenty four hours to lift-off, the port side lacked its final top coat and both sides were still unnamed. I used the quiet of the closing day to paint the letters on the starboard side, knowing that we would all be up at the crack of dawn on the following day.

Christian Bugge returns to the Indian Ocean, ten tonnes lighter than when she was hauled out, sodden with sea water

Our dilapidated dory acts as ferryboat. In the background, one of the island schooners is under repair on the slipway.

John was on site at 5.30a.m. By mid morning the yard was a hive of activity as the men prepared the site for the steel giant which would raise our old lady from terra firma. The resident ants of the past eleven months were in for quite a shock!

I applied the 'E' of Bugge at 1.00p.m., my nerves on edge as the scaffolding was pulled down around me, making the flimsy section that still held my weight, vibrate and sway in the wind.

Miraculously the show went on and at 4.30p.m. Christian Bugge was raised from her resting place and dangled aloft while hidden crevices were now revealed and touched up by willing hands. Spectators gasped as the clutch on the crane slipped slightly, but the operator was in control and within minutes, Christian Bugge was afloat in the Indian Ocean.

John and Andy were glowing with the feeling of a job well done, and that evening they glowed even more with sparkling liquid refreshment and sumptuous buffet, laid on by friends who were as excited as we were by the achievement.

Work went on as usual next day, this time accompanied by an easy rolling motion. Three days later the planks had swelled and Christian Bugge was not taking any water. We lifted in the engine and towed her to a safe anchorage close to the shore between Libertas, a converted German wartime fishing boat, and Wallaby, an ugly Dutch canal boat. Here our dory came into its own, working as ferry from the cluttered foreshore where rusty metal, broken bottles and slimy rocks impeded our progress, causing us all to fall at some time during the next few months.

It was difficult to find enough shade from the tropical sun to concentrate on the lettering.

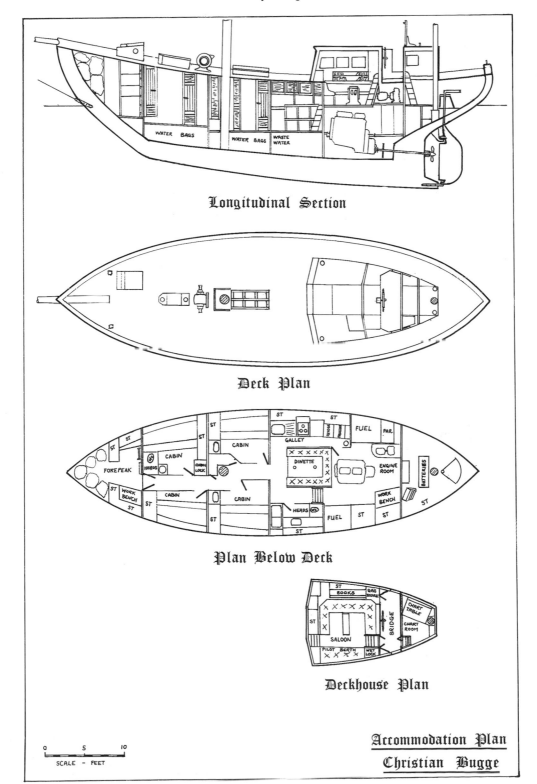

Longitudinal Section

Deck Plan

Plan Below Deck

Deckhouse Plan

SCALE - FEET

Accommodation Plan
Christian Bugge

John and Andy take a breather.

Jimmy works on a wire rope splice.

Andy constructs the pinrail around the mast.

Time off for tea and socialising.

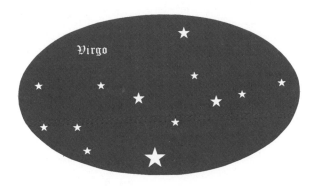

A Change Of Plan

Eleven months of working on the outside of Christian Bugge had given us a bronzed and weathered look. Now that she was floating happily in Victoria Harbour, there was nothing for it but to retreat to the dingy, cavernous interior of her hull. Our healthy tans disappeared and our eyes became saucers as we scraped and cleaned, cleaned and scraped. Meanwhile Eric, an ancient skinny Seychellois, built solid if not elegant bulkheads. We had deliberately kept the inside bare until this moment to avoid unnecessary weight at the time of the crane lift.

Out came the drawings for the interior design and we forged ahead with the grand plan.

With so much space to fill, we had decided to have as many separate areas as possible so that each member of the two families could keep some privacy. Four double cabins were planned for the forward section of the boat, with work area and sail storage in the bows and small heads just aft of this. The galley would remain where it was originally situated in the mid section, but was redesigned to incorporate a dinette with seating for eight people. The main heads would also be in the mid section and would include a shower and cupboard space for provisions. The saloon was to be in the aft section of the ship, occupying roughly the same area of deck as the old aluminium wheelhouse, but extending below deck level to within a few inches of the top of the engine. Although we were going to be sitting over the engine, full standing headroom would be possible in the main section of the engine room. With careful planning, we could keep the height of the saloon/deckhouse to a minimum - important for aesthetics and also for heavy weather. We decided to have the helmsman's position at deck level, aft of the saloon where there would be some protection from seas and where there was good all- round vision. The watchkeeper's back would be further protected by the chartroom which was to follow the line of the deckhouse. It would occupy the curve of the stern section above a rope storage locker in the engine room. All living areas would have full standing headroom but only the saloon and the chartroom would boast a 'sea view' through rectangular windows. The rest of the ship would obtain diffused daylight from prismatic decklights set in brass surrounds flush with the deck. Many of the original decklights were broken and would need replacing - another job for our buyer in U.K.

While most of us burrowed in the bowels of Bugge, Andy was sweating off his last spare pounds of flesh by wrestling with the main mast. Once the topmost eleven foot section had been scarfed on and the trestle trees completed, varnishing began. Of course it stood to reason that whenever a fresh coat was being applied, a few grim clouds would appear from nowhere and a sharp shower would send the varnisher scurrying for the polythene cover. By the time he had covered the last of the sixty five feet, the sun would be turning the shower to steam!

Where, oh where did the days go?

Iain returned from England in August, and within three weeks of his arrival, a unit in the Seychelles Army staged a mutiny. The mutineers took over the Radio Station and broadcast frightening threats to blow up all the major services in Victoria. Complete curfew was imposed yet again and this time Seychellois blood was spilled. From our veranda we could see palls of black smoke rising from the town as the patter of firing took effect. Tanzanian soldiers appeared in trucks on the airport road and we felt sad for this beautiful little country. President René had been visiting an outer island when the trouble began, but he finally managed to return to Mahé to broadcast a reassuring message to his nation. As his loyal forces took control again, we wondered just what had been at the root of the trouble. Why should brother turn against brother? No doubt the mutineers were given stern punishment, but the worst aftermath was the expression on the faces of the people. They became tight lipped, afraid to go out after dark, and above all bitter. It was evident that there had been more deaths than the government cared to acknowledge.

Once the drama was all over, we were relieved to return to the boatyard and find that Christian Bugge was undamaged. The children collected spent cartridges as souvenirs.

We were due to set out for the African continent in November so as to avoid the worst of the cyclone season which was reputed to peak between December and February in the Indian Ocean. Finally we had to admit defeat and hold a conference to express verbally what we all knew in our hearts. We were well behind schedule. At this stage we kidded ourselves that we were perhaps only six months out in our estimate but, like all our figures, this was later to be doubled. Most of our friends were not at all surprised. Wearily, we made arrangements to stay on in Seychelles with the aim of leaving as soon as possible in 1983.

John's contract came to an end in October and Andy's at the beginning of November. Neither could be renewed again. Pat and I had given in notice for Half Term, also in November, and since the posts had already been filled, we could not snatch our jobs back this time. The financial position was grim, but on November 5th 1982 the main mast and our spirits were raised. As the mast swayed above Christian Bugge, there was a frantic hour while the heel was shaved and revarnished to fit the step. I never did discover whose measurements were at fault!

Andy was keen to start on the galvanised wire rigging which needed expert splicing. We were lucky enough to find an old timer who had worked in the Royal Fleet Auxiliary, and after a demonstration, Andy was able to carry on with assistance from Jimmy, our 'boat boy'. Splices were covered with a soft mixture of white lead and tallow, parcelled with canvas and served. Eighteen months later these were still found to be in excellent condition. Ratlines were fixed between the capping shroud and the forward main shroud.

We tried to keep our spirits up by relaxing at least one evening each week at our folk singing rehearsals. John and Andy had formed a group called 'Creaking Capstan' because they both enjoyed singing sea shanties. Later they expanded their repertoire to take in sea songs and other folk ditties. The formation of the group changed as families came and went. Mary Romanos gave us the big sound of the accordion but we changed this for the accomplished violin playing of an Australian girl called Sally Banks when Mary left the island. Mike Kingsley gave weight to the male voices and even Ron stayed with the group for a while, giving us the benefit of his distinctive rasping tones. Lucy and Joan formed their own offshoot and became 'The Windlassies'. I sang or played the recorder or flute wherever necessary and Pat was very good at making coffee. Iain usually read a book as far away as possible, unless anything edible put in an appearance. These evenings served as good unwinding sessions after the difficulties of the day.

By December an entirely new set of problems had arisen.

Our house was rented for us by the government. Since we no longer qualified for such help, we had to move out. Pat and John were in a similar position. Fortunately we were both able to gain a brief respite by 'house warming' for expatriates who were on leave for the festive season but we faced the prospect of having to move aboard Christian Bugge in January.

One Sunday before Christmas, Pat and I sat quietly varnishing cupboard doors for the galley while Joan and Lucy played 'catch' in the garden. Suddenly there was an anguished cry from the frangipani tree which was home base. Joan got to her feet with a strangely mis-shapen wrist and a look of disbelief on her face. I drove Pat's ramshackle Mini while Pat cradled the arm to cushion the jolting on the rough road from Beauvallon to Victoria. By the time we reached the hospital, the shock was wearing off and Joan was in agony. She bore it well along with the extra suffering caused by having to push her in a wheelchair to the Radiology Department for an X-ray. There were further delays while we waited for the surgeon to return from the beach, but at last the arm was in plaster. Because of the nature of the break, there was concern that it might be difficult to set the bone in its correct position, but after another spell in the operating theatre next morning, all seemed to be well and Joan was allowed home. Her main concern was that she had had nothing to eat for twenty four hours! Pat's main concern was how to entertain such an active child with quiet pastimes! Six weeks of no swimming, no running, no climbing, was a devastating blow to someone like Joan.

Christmas came and went. John and Pat were unable to housewarm for friends any longer, so they moved in with us.

In our blackest moods we foresaw gradual starvation, for we had surprisingly

Andy and Iain work on the scarf joint for the top section of the main mast.

little left of the lump sum we had received in lieu of air fares, and none of us had a job. We could not afford to send the girls to school any more and shopping became a nightmare of indecision. To top it all, Immigration were keeping a close watch on us, now that we only qualified for a temporary permit to stay in the Republic.

It seemed as if we were running down a dark alley towards a dead end with barbed wire on either side. Somehow we kept going. Pat and I held little sales on the veranda to bring in a few rupees. We got rid of anything we did not need on the boat, surplus pots and pans, bedding, curtains, lamp shades, toys, books, games. Second hand electrical goods always fetch a good price in remote places, so we sold a hand mixer, blender, iron and fan. I had already sold our fridge/freezer, washing machine and hi-fi set when we left the house in November.

We scurried round in an effort to make Christian Bugge habitable for the 19th January, my birthday. That day is etched in my mind as one of the most miserable in my life. It was hot even for the Tropics, with a sultry haze and warm drizzle. We spent the morning in a frenzy of packing and cleaning because our friends, Don and Gay Stone were expected back at midday. Their car drew up just as we were sweeping out the last dead cockroaches and lizard droppings. They looked cool and relaxed, whilst I felt like a piece of self basting roast pork. It took the rest of the daylight hours to ferry the clutter aboard and stow some of it out of

Lucy and Joan could not wait for their bunks to be ready.

sight. Andy struggled to fit the canvas pipe cots while the children's eyes grew heavy with sleep. John was still working on the wiring so that we could have light and water. The heat below decks grew more and more oppressive as it was intensified by toil. At about 10.00p.m. we managed to perch on beer crates for a glass of wine and piece of cake by way of celebration. None of us had the strength to go and shower at the Yacht Club, but since we all smelled the same, it did not seem to matter. Because his cabin was not finished, Iain had to sleep on a sunbed in the galley, surrounded by debris. We all slumbered heavily that night.

We had dreaded living amongst the mess. However, a few weeks after the move, we had to admit that it made life easier in some respects. We were able to sort out our priorities because we lived on top of the problems and there was also much less travelling involved. Approximately half the boat was habitable on moving day, so with seven people constantly searching for a space to call their own, there was great incentive to complete dinette, main heads and saloon.

We survived January. Then in February our guardian angel tossed us a few crumbs of comfort which we pounced on hungrily. Pat secured a job teaching O-level English to adults at evening classes - six hours per week. Unbelievably, within two weeks she was also offered a full time post at a National Youth Service Camp, again teaching English. Since the evening classes began at 4.30p.m. there was no way that Pat could do both, so she accepted the full time job whilst I managed to talk the director of the Polytechnic into allowing me to tackle the evening classes. At the same time I obtained regular work at the International School as their supply teacher, and I also took on several pupils for private tuition. I went from job to job like a zombie.

A typical day went something like this.

Pat and I rose at 5.45a.m. with the first suspicion of dawn. After breakfast I collected the dirty washing from the seven of us and at 6.30 ferried Pat to the Yacht Club in our inflatable dinghy. This five minute trip across the harbour was pleasant in the early morning sun. I liked the leisurely atmosphere of the town as it slowly began to swing into action for the day. I tied up the dinghy, said goodbye to Pat who hurried off to catch the NYS minibus, and lugged my washing to the outside sinks provided for yachties. There I usually encountered the night watchman, who was clearing out last night's sour empties from the bar. Sometimes he was to be found sitting on a beer crate, devouring his breakfast - fish curry and rice. The washing usually took me half an hour if it was straightforward. I stuffed a pair of underpants in the plug hole and cursed silently every time it came out. The wringing was the worst part of the job. I returned to Christian Bugge, already wet with sweat, feeling as if I had been wrung out myself. If the International School found they needed me to take a class, the secretary would come down to the boatyard and hail me from the shore between 7.30 and 8.00. If I was below deck, or if the boatyard was having a particularly noisy morning, it took her a long time to attract my attention. I then had to make myself presentable and walk the half mile to school which started at 7.50 and finished at 12.20. At 1.00p.m. I taught English to an Italian boy, and an Indian boy, each for half an hour. At 3.00 I drove two miles to teach a Korean girl for one hour and here I was presented with two solitary fried eggs by the attentive mother. Luckily I am very fond of eggs, but I think some Europeans would have found the prospect of unaccompanied eggs in the middle of a hot afternoon, a daunting one. Mr and Mrs Moon and their adorable daughters Mi Jin, Mi Rang, Haing Jin became very good friends to us in those last months. I left their house at 4.00 with just enough time to put a comb through my hair before the evening class at 4.30. Sometimes I met Pat returning from work and we would have a short debate about what we could eat that evening. Shark steaks were popular because they were very cheap. Often the men were left to do the shopping in between their mucky jobs on the boat. They also took time off to

Mi Jin Moon takes charge of the barbecue.

do English and maths with the girls, who missed out on co-ordinated routine during those busy months.

At the evening class I made a big effort to appear cool and relaxed for my twenty students, most of whom were Seychellois people, aged 20 - 50, desperately trying to improve their written English. At first they were reluctant to make any oral contribution to the lessons as their education had been very formal, but they warmed to the idea as the weeks went by. When I left the group seven months later I felt that I had learned a great deal about the character of the Seychellois. More importantly I hoped that their vocabulary and experience of the English language had been extended, even if they never got as far as the O-level exam.

On one afternoon each week I took a recorder group on board Christian Bugge. Friends of Lucy and Joan thought it was marvellous to have a nautical environment for their lesson, and there was an added bonus in that if parents were not too prompt, they would have time to play at climbing the rigging or diving off the side, before they went home. These sessions were great fun. Sometimes a friend would turn up at 4.00 with a cake, encouraging the men to down tools and join the tea party. We made a pleasing tableau in the softening light of late afternoon.

After supper at 7.00 Pat and I usually had marking or preparation to do for the following day. Often there were two shower excursions so that by coffee time the whole crew was shiny and clean. Occasionally someone in the Yacht Club would take pity on us and buy drinks for one of the shower parties which made the rest green with envy. By now we were managing to live on 400 Rupees (£40) per week for the seven of us, and in the Seychelles that was good going. We drank only water, tea or coffee and ate mostly fish and rice, local vegetables such as aubergines and cucumbers, bread, jam, homemade cakes or puddings, and of course bananas which were usually plentiful, very cheap and ten times more succulent than the floury textured varieties which appear in British greengrocers.

For a time we laid off all our Seychelles workers, but as a little money came in we took one or two back for some carpentry work which Andy and John could not undertake, mainly because there was not enough time in the day.

For several weeks in February and March, John was unable to undertake very much at all. Misfortune struck our commune once again. We all enjoyed Scottish Dancing and did not think of it as hazardous until John's knee gave way with a broken cartilage. He spent two weeks in hospital and was incapacitated for much longer. With our kind of luck we began to wonder if we would ever make it as far as the harbour entrance, let alone the coast of England.

By April, the deckhouse and chartroom were weatherproof with vertical hardwood planking and cambered roof of three quarter inch plywood, sheathed in fibreglass The mizzen mast proudly balanced her taller partner and the main boom and bowsprit had been heaved aboard. When fitted, the boom only just cleared the mizzen, but we confidently proclaimed we had planned it that way. However, we had to admit defeat over the length of the bowsprit. After much heaving and straining to push it through the leathered opening at the bow, we came to the conclusion that it would be just as good, if not better, with six inches

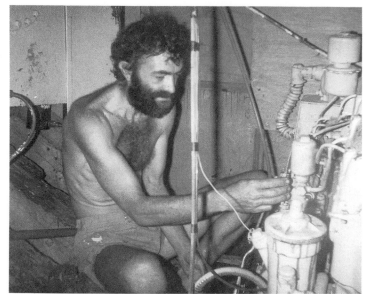

Andy gives the engine a final check.

lopped off the lower end. Andy fetched the saw.

Now we began to look like a real ship. We acknowledged the admiring glances of men who longed to take adventure by the horns as we had but whose wives knew better than to let their dreams become reality!

Many of the jobs completed in 1982 now needed redoing, not the least of these being the antifouling. Before we could slip her on the yard's new cradles, we had to have our engine connected. This meant a trial run or two, so one drowsy afternoon, we nonchalantly cast off our encrusted shore warps, and started the Gardner 5LW. Christian Bugge was in no hurry to go anywhere because we had succeeded in winding the rope to our mooring buoy round the propeller. Definitely not a good start. Luckily, not many people were around to notice. A few minutes under water with an air bottle put things right and we moved gracefully out of the harbour. We were so excited to find that we could actually move after almost two years that we could not contain ourselves. The ecstatic whoops of joy from the children attracted attention from passing pleasure boats. Some contained friends returning to harbour after their Sunday's boozing and snoozing on the tiny off-shore islands. They shouted their joy for us and we felt complacent.

As we neared the lighthouse guarding the reef near the harbour entrance, smoke began to issue from the engine room.

"Only the paint burning off the exhaust pipes" said Andy convincingly.

Five minutes later it was almost impossible to go below for smoke. We switched off the engine and anchored on the edge of the channel within a stone's throw of the reef. It was 4.00p.m. so we put the kettle on and sought solace in a cup of tea while the fumes were dispersing. We tried to make it look as if it were the most natural thing in all the world to anchor in the channel for a cup of tea. We continued waving cheerily but were desperately trying to think of a way out of our predicament, for at this time there was a 6.00p.m. curfew at sea, following the army mutiny of the previous August. Happily, rescue came in the shape of an old whaler which was capable of towing us back to our mooring. We slipped in through the harbour entrance only five minutes late.

The explanation for the overheating was this. When the heat exchanger unit came from the factory, the open ends were blanked off with red plastic dust covers. When the engine was assembled in U.K., a hose pipe was clipped to the heat exchanger and one plastic cover was inadvertently left in place.

We spent six days on the slip for routine maintenance.

On returning to our mooring I began the repainting of the topsides and the men worked towards the sailing trials.

The great day came, towards the end of July - a sultry Sunday enabling normal folk with weekday jobs to accompany us.

That first froth of white sail in dazzling sunshine was an agreeable sight. We eased Christian Bugge out of the harbour under engine and then hoisted mizzen, main, staysail and No.1 jib in a gentle breeze. Amazingly, there were no major hitches on our twelve mile trip. Our loyal friends were able to raise bottles to their lips with no danger of them being jolted out of their hands.

The very next weekend, we entered the prestige event in the Seychelles calendar - the Beauvallon Regatta. We were given an old gaffer's handicap, but our enthusiastic crew leaped from side to side, in a Force 5 - 6 wind, putting the old girl about as if she were a racing machine! The four hour race was not without its drama. After the second mark, we were bunched up with some smaller boats looking for the third which, we felt sure should have appeared by this time. Other

John has a bird's eye view of the crew from the trestle trees.

skippers were anxiously scanning the water for the orange buoy. Jimmy could contain himself no longer and shinned up the rigging. He spotted the mark just as we drew abreast of it and we reached across towards it. Those who had been ahead of us were now forced to gybe round and chase us, which meant we had jumped a few places. The long windward leg was still to come, but somehow we held onto the race and crossed the line in second place after breaking our pin rail around the foot of the mast in an unexpected gust only 200 metres from the finish. On handicap we took the trophy. Those who had shaken their heads sadly over our big ideas for Christian Bugge now came forward to be the first to congratulate us. We were jubilant. That weekend we had touched eight knots in gusty conditions over flat water, so we had every reason to be satisfied with Christian Bugge's performance which demonstrated a powerful, well balanced rig. Now we had to start building up the muscles of the two families to man the sheets and halyards, all worked by block and tackle in the traditional way.

With only a little sigh, we resumed the work schedule, confident that we really would sail out of Victoria Harbour towards the idyllic islands of the Amirantes and adventures unknown, before the end of 1983.

Andy, Jimmy and William enjoy the challenge of the Beauvallon race after two years of work on shore

Iain poses with the Regatta Trophy

Libra

Departure At Last

For the second year running, we were up against the cyclone season, so we could not afford to sit back on our laurels. Work went on at an even more frantic pace as we aimed for late September or early October.

Little favours and kindnesses helped us through the last fraught weeks and one particular gift sticks in my memory. Iain was called over to Libertas one day, by Hans who acted as captain and caretaker for the German owner. He had a large tuna fish for us. Iain motored over in the inflatable and collected the twenty five pound fish while Hans watched from the deck. As Iain lifted it up towards willing hands on Christian Bugge, it slipped out of his grasp into the water. There was just time for the mocking words of Hans to be heard, before Iain followed the tuna like lightning, diving deeply to come up under the sinking fish. He struggled to lift it clear of the surface and glanced at Hans, glad that he had saved face. We were also glad because a tuna of that size provided us with five or six meals.

I continued teaching through September with one memorable occasion. As I negotiated the ladder to set off for school, I missed a handhold and fell back into the water. Desperately, I tried to hold my bag of books above sea level as I screeched for someone to come and take it. Having deliberately started out early, I was livid at being in that bedraggled state. My rescuers, on the other hand, found my plight amusing.

September was also the month when I blotted my copybook as a law abiding citizen. I was stopped for speeding on my way back from Mi Jin's lesson, and to cap it all, my Seychelles driving licence was six months out of date! The summons was served from a police launch and the case was due to come up in the middle of October. I'm sorry to say, I quite forgot to tell the policeman that I was leaving the island!

We began saying goodbyes and taking on stores to last us to Durban.

Constantly we were asked when we were leaving and our answers were always non committal - "Quite soon now", or "When we are ready". Some friends said goodbye regularly just in case we took them by surprise and slipped away when nobody was looking.

The weather did not help. It was awful - wet and windy for weeks on end, which was most unlike the halcyon days of other Septembers we had known. One gale picked up real speed for a few hours, so that we had difficulty in staying on our feet. The roaring wind snatched sheets of plywood and tossed them into the sea. One of the heavy poles which held up our awning, snapped like matchwood before we could take down the billowing canvas. Rainstorm after rainstorm prevented us from painting the decks to eliminate the last few leaks. It was not that we had many drips, but those we did have were most inconvenient. The one over the cooker often extinguished the front burner, and I never did get used to the one in the loo. No matter which way I leaned, I could never avoid the steady flow of droplets. It's a wonder we didn't all suffer from constipation!

There were several offers of help in those last few weeks. The day Jennie came to paint the bulwarks, work in the boatyard came to a halt, for she was top-less. It was just as well Pat and I hadn't carried on that way for the two and a half years we spent visiting the boatyard! It was Jennie who went to the top of the mast, fully clothed this time, to give Andy his farewell kiss two days before we left. She was always a trend setter.

Mr Moon, our Korean friend, brought his family down to say goodbye and gave us rice, tuna, and soy sauce. In his scrambled English he told us that a teacher has the same status as a king in Korea, and that he would never forget us.

On October 6th we thought we might leave on the 8th, on the 7th we decided to go on the 10th, and on the 8th Martin Shaw arrived on the scene. He was one of a crew of six who had set out from England in November 1982 to go round the world East about via Cape Verde and South Africa. Their adventure was brought to an untimely close in the Amirantes. One minute they were scudding along in the fresh evening breeze, and the next minute their boat was lodged on the reef close to the coralline island of Astove. Here the six of them spent two months with the seven islanders, waiting for a boat to take them to Mahé. Having sunk all their resources along with the boat, Martin and his friends were penniless and looking for options. Martin approached us for a passage to Durban where he had other contacts in mind to help him on his way from there. Pat and I were dubious about taking a new personality into the group at this late stage, but he tried so hard to make a good impression that we decided to take the risk. He found himself making storm shutters before the day was out.

October 11th dawned, and we were determined to put Mahé behind us before midnight. Andy was looking gaunt with the strain of past weeks and even now wrestled with a wayward Lister generator.

Late in the day we let go our shore warps, swung out into the harbour from the Libertas buoy and hauled up the inflatable. Dusk was settling on Trois Frères mountain and I had only a dim impression of the few stalwart friends determined to see us go. A hooter disturbed the quiet of evening and a lump came into my throat. As we sailed out of the harbour entrance, I clung to the starboard light to keep the wires connected for the benefit of the Seychelles Navy who watched us

Early morning sun shows our ship heavily laden and almost ready for departure.

go. Lucy and Joan were already opening the package labelled, 'Not to be opened until the BIG DAY', given by a thoughtful friend. All kinds of goodies were inside, destined to keep them busy for many days. There were suggestions and scraps for sewing, ideas for pictures and diaries, a jigsaw, plastic bowl, post cards, sweets, and other edible treats.

The gentle South East breeze enabled us to take a last lingering look at Mahé as we rounded the Northern end and headed across Beauvallon Bay where we had spent many happy hours during our four years in the Seychelles. The low thump of a disco beat drifted across the calm water and I imagined the Seychelles dancing scene at Takamaka 2. I chuckled over one friend's advice on the art of Sega dancing - "Pretend you've got a cut foot" he recommended. This really did work. Having achieved the basic cut foot rhythm, it was no problem to add bottom wiggling and arm waggling in sympathy with one's partner.

Mahé began to recede. We assembled some tins and called the resulting sludge a meal. Somehow it wasn't important that first night. The enormity of the moment of departure had made me feel tiny and querulous. This fine feeling was soon replaced by one in my guts which pumped my meal, now even more of a sludge, upwards. Pat had a similar problem, no doubt encouraged by extreme fatigue.

The night watches began with Andy and I taking the 12.00a.m. - 3.00a.m. The novelty of it made us forget to feel tired. The gentle swell of the Indian Ocean buoyed our elation at being underway, and only gradually did the fingers of sleep touch our eyes as we sat hand in hand at the stern, marvelling at the night. Pat and John took over at 3.00a.m. Iain and Martin were on the breakfast watch, 6.00 - 9.00.

By dawn, the wind had freshened to a comfortable force 3 - 4 from the South East, giving us an estimated speed of 4 - 5 knots. A hush settled over the boat as each one of us came to terms with departure. I felt a sense of awe and fear of the unknown, conscious that we had not had enough sailing trials. Andy and John were exhausted but relieved to be away from land. Pat must have felt somewhat downcast and uncertain for she was not a natural sailor. The two girls hardly seemed to have noticed that we had left and were quite oblivious of the unfamiliar rolling motion. Iain fought continual nausea by remaining on deck where he could frown at the horizon. Martin must have had very mixed feelings. After all, he had said goodbye to close friends and was now heading back towards the reef which had brought disaster and an end to his independence. If this bothered him, he certainly did not let it show. He was doggedly cheerful and willing to help with absolutely anything that needed doing. Because neither Andy nor John had any experience of long distance cruising, they were very glad of Martin's advice.

At 0800 hours the echo sounder showed that we had cleared the Seychelles Bank. Andy took the first sunsight and streamed the Walker log. Only 15,000 miles to go.

Scorpius

Hazardous Beginning via The Amirantes

At dawn on the second day, Iain scanned the ocean from the trestle trees, thirty seven feet up the mast. Desroches Island in the Amirantes was fifteen miles away, bearing North North West. We gybed twice in a light South Easterly wind in order to stem the strong Westerly current and headed in to cross the Desroches Bank three miles North of Pointes Hélène. We dropped anchor off the settlement in an idyllic setting of clear sky and crystal water, with coconut palms and casuarina pines rising in profusion from the kidney shaped island.

The manager of the settlement motored out to welcome us and later guided us round his small domain. He told us he was employed by the Island Development Corporation which runs many of the outer islands for the Seychelles Republic. Of necessity he wore numerous hats. He was boss of the Sawmill and Copra Industry, manager of the shop, doctor of the clinic, accountant for island affairs, as well as friend and confidant to the small group of workers on Desroches. He showed us his turkeys, chickens, doves, and one venerable peacock, allegedly put there by Mancham, deposed President of Seychelles.

With pleasure, I drank in the quiet unhurried atmosphere of the lush island. We visited the sawmill which was the managers pride and joy, and gazed at the old disused crusher for the production of coconut oil. It consisted of a thatched round house, open at the sides, with a stone trough in the middle served by a large wooden funnel into which the coconuts were placed. To operate the crusher and thereby collect the valuable oil, an ox would have been tied to the central contraption and made to walk in endless circles. The manager assured us that little was needed to restore this to working order and talked as if he would like to see the industry revived, but I doubt whether he could make it a viable proposition.

Our two days in Desroches came to an end and it was time to raise the mainsail again.

Martin and I hauled on the peak halyard while John and Iain heaved on the throat halyard. We were learning the importance of working as a team, so as to keep the gaff at the correct angle and thus minimise jamming. Andy remained in the steering position where he could give orders and watch for trailing ropes. I enjoyed the rhythmic effort of hauling up that heavy gaff and feeling the wind over the bows, snatching the sails to and fro in joyous invitation to be away. Up came the anchor and out flew the staysail to take us on a beam reach through the West passage in the Desroches reef. As we cleared the West end of the island and hoisted the mizzen and No. 1 jib, I felt the bows lift over the waves with the extra power.

Before long we were in the company of a host of dolphins, not just a family playing in the bow wave, but dolphins as far as the eye could see. We all jostled onto the foredeck for a better view of their antics, gasping as they criss-crossed in fast formations under the bows. The more extrovert dolphins performed repeated triple somersaults in a cloud of spray while others were content to curve gently out of the water in twos and threes. Their forty five minute display seemed to me to be an offer of companionship and a good omen for our travels.

As the day wore on we went about onto a port tack, making about five and a half knots in a Southerly Force Three, but by nightfall the wind was dying away. We ran the engine for two hours in the lull, to make sure we cleared the island of Marie Louise, but as the new watchkeepers went on deck at 2100 hours a fresh South Easterly was gathering speed. The course was altered to 230 degrees compass so as to pass between Alphonse and Des Noeufs. We bowled along at six knots in the blackness, constantly checking our navigation, aware that if we miscalculated or were taken by an unusual current, we would recognise the reef only by the jarring and rending in the hull. As dawn streaked the sky we spied Alphonse bearing 130 degrees, somewhat closer than our navigation had lead us to expect!

During Monday, the seventh day out of Mahe, the wind continued to increase until we were ploughing along with No. 2 jib and reefed mainsail in a wild night.

Martin leads the way on Desroches.

Anchored off Cosmoledo Atoll.

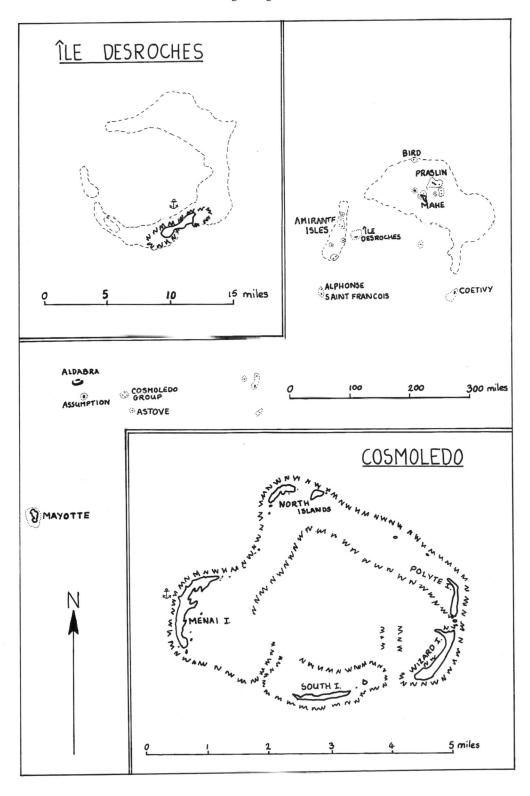

Joan and Lucy slept soundly down below as the wind began to howl its madness in the rigging. We dropped the mizzen and reefed the staysail but still we seemed to be overpowered by gusts which were approaching Force Eight. At 0300 hours Pat was rudely awakened by grimy bilge water sloshing around in her bunk and the galley was awash with black slime. We had been so busy with the sails, we had not given the bilges a thought, and now they were reminding us that we should have pumped them dry. Still mucky from the weeks prior to our departure, they disgorged their filth each time Christian Bugge heeled at a steep angle. As we tramped through the galley our feet picked up the grime and spread it all over the boat, but we didn't have time to worry about that. At 0400 hours the rain sheeted down and our mainsail was still catching too much wind, so it was all hands on deck to put in a second reef. I clung to the steering wheel and followed shouted instructions while Andy, Iain, John and Martin staggered forward attached to safety lines, to cheat the wind of some sail. Lowering the boom onto the gallows proved almost impossible, even with the engine running to keep our nose into the wind. When they thought they had tamed the boom by sheeting it into the crutch, Andy climbed onto the coachroof to wrestle with the reefing gear. Suddenly the boom jerked out of position and caught him across the ribs. He somersaulted onto the deck, badly winded but feeling himself lucky not to have been thrown into the turbulent sea. Warm as it was, it would have shown little mercy for a sailor separated from his vessel. Somehow we finished reefing the sail.

The wind slackened a little with daylight but the waves were mischievous. Iain and I stayed on deck to enjoy the frothy seascape. We catalogued the waves into 'sheer strake skimmers', 'bulwark bashers', and 'rail rovers'. The rail rovers were the most dramatic and could easily turn into 'deckhouse dunkers'! In brilliant sunlight we could appreciate the blustery weather and forget the nightmare of the early hours. Fortunately all of us had recovered from the sea sickness that plagued us in the first day or two. That as well as the bilge swill would have been too much to bear. As it was, Pat had to roam the boat for a vacant place to rest her head because she could not sleep in her own bunk.

With the wind gusting forty knots again, we were anxiously scanning the horizon for the coral atoll of Cosmoledo which promised a chance to dry out and recuperate. We had shipped a lot of sea water which had seeped into clothes and bedding. When Andy spotted Wizard Island on our port bow, we celebrated with a cup of hot soup which took little time to prepare and much much longer to transfer from saucepan, to cup, to eager hands as Christian Bugge lurched over the waves. She rode the bucking seas with joyous abandon. One moment the starboard windows would be buried in a cloud of spray, only to soar skywards again as the breaking wave passed by and tipped us into a trough.

The excitement seemed to stir Lucy and Joan into singing Christmas carols to the tape recorder all morning. The fact that they had to hang on tight to stop themselves and the tape recorder from sliding across the saloon while books and magazines rained down upon them, did not matter to them at all. The words of 'Silent night' were sprinkled incongruously upon the wind.

We anchored off the settlement at Menai Island, one of the seven in the Cosmoledo atoll.

Martin nobly attacked the galley floor with Tepol and a scrubbing brush, while Pat began the grim task of cleaning her bunk and the cavity below which was filled with personal possessions. This turned out to be the good part of the day.

After a meal and a celebratory bottle of wine, we sat basking in the glow of achievement. Our eyes began to close at coffee time until Iain broke into our reveries with a hoarse cry, "The dinghy's broken loose!" We rushed to the stern and stared at our inflatable hurrying off into the night with a Force five wind and two knot current. All we could do was take its bearing, up anchor and chase after it. We tried. The anchor winch proved stubborn, coming up at snail's pace in little jerks - obviously air in the hydraulics again. Why did it have to happen now? The look-outs lost sight of the dinghy and we were still working on the anchor. It must have taken us twenty minutes to break free and on top of all this we had to connect the macerator pump to the engine to provide the cooling system, because the pump impeller on the Gardner had broken.

We headed out into the wild night on a fool's errand. Bodies were posted along the bulwarks and the searchlight panned the ocean. Nothing. We returned wet, silent and cold, trying to forgive the knot maker who shall remain nameless. Thank goodness we did not sell the fibreglass dory and small outboard engine. Tomorrow's job would be to do some repair work on it and devise a good system for lifting it into the water.

The settlement area of Cosmoledo was arid and sparse. A few houses, some livestock, racks of drying fish and baby booby birds were the only things to be seen. The man in charge told us that the manager was away on a three day fishing trip and left us to explore the island by ourselves. We headed into the interior which consisted mainly of salt pools and mangrove. Ranks of crabs glared at us from the dry undergrowth and every so often, one of them rushed at our feet and made the girls squeal. Like a dog with two tails, Martin boasted of crab conquests on Astove where he had been forced to practise survival as a shipwrecked mariner. He assured us that we needed crabs as bait for our fishing, and enlisted the help of Andy and Iain. The rest of us had a good laugh watching them being outwitted by these large crustaceans. Time and time again the machete guillotined the air and the cry went up, "I've got one", but somehow the crab would elude its pursuer and Martin would be left with a single claw. Coconuts proved an easier target for the machete and the sweet water provided consolation as we completed our tour.

The rest of our stay was devoted to chores. Having watched the insistent flap of the sails in light airs, we realised that chafe was likely to become a problem. We persuaded Lucy and Joan to get busy with some strands of of rope cut to short lengths of about ten inches. They knotted the strands around a taut length of twine to produce some passable baggywrinkle which we could wind round the rigging. In return, John, Iain and I allowed ourselves to be coerced into playing 'The great game of Britain', a board game in which one has to travel all over U.K. by rail,

Anchored off Assumption.

Lucy, Joan and Pat making the most of the freshwater on   *One of the three inhabitants.*
Assumption Island

trying to visit certain places of interest before dashing back to London. It reminded us of the pace of life awaiting us at the end of the voyage.

It was a short hop to Assumption, an uninhabited island once the source of rich bounty for guano hunters. The deserted settlement had an eerie quality. Tractors, generators and other machinery stood forgotten in sheds. Bellows and charcoal were ready for the fire in the blacksmith's shop. In the clinic, pills and medicines littered the table. Papers and files spilled onto the floor of the office. Large bags of salt sat in store sheds. Beer bottles stood guard in the timber houses where doors swung to and fro in the wind. The small cluster of graves recorded only two names - Francis Bristol, died 1931 and Captain Savvy, died 1952. The ceramic flowers on an unnamed grave showed bright colours through the casuarina pine needles which formed a springy mat over the island.

When three domestic pigs were sighted, the Christian Bugge crew licked their lips in anticipation of barbecued pork and tried to herd them into a corner. Fortunately the pigs still knew how to run and later, when we saw the sow at close quarters, we discovered she had about as much flesh on her as a greyhound. What kept those pigs alive we will never know, for the only other living things to be seen on that island were ants, flies and mosquitoes. Presumably the guano industry had caused many of the endemic species of animal life to disappear. Only the wind stirred the strange silence of the island.

We barbecued some tuna in the shade of the old boat sheds and cooled our skin in the blue bay. To freshen up we moved to large rainwater tanks, courtesy of the guano hunters, where Lucy and Joan found some watering cans and acted as bath attendants. After two weeks of salt, my skin was grateful for the touch of fresh water. With buckets and bowls, Pat and I set up a washing station and pum-

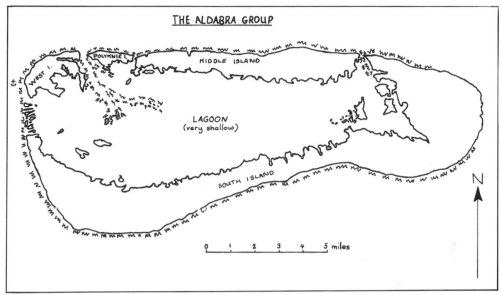

melled all the clothes while the men searched for scrap metal which might be of use to us. We tied line between trees and finally lugged the dry washing back to the beach. The mosquitoes began to home in on us, so we wandered along the broken pier to watch a Tiger Fish darting from the depths to the surface, to snatch one of the crabs from the wall. He crunched it up and spat out a few indigestible bits before retreating to the bottom to repeat the procedure. The crabs got very excited and seemed to jostle each other, as if for a better view, regardless of the fact that they were likely to be eaten.

We were sorry to leave the island which had become our very own kingdom, but eager to glimpse Aldabra, the largest raised coral atoll in the world, only thirty miles away. I had long yearned to see this strange place that was designated a World Heritage Site in 1982. Prior to Independence in 1976 it had been rescued from the claws of British politicians who had tried to retain it as part of a separate British Indian Ocean Territory, with a view to constructing a strategic Air and Naval Base there. Now it is run by the Seychelles Island Foundation which employs a small team of people to protect the marine reserves for scientific study.

We spotted the low forbidding coastline in the early hours of October 24th and skirted the North coast in the company of frigate birds above and sharks below. The sharp edges of the coral thrusting up through the surf gave off sinister vibrations and made me shudder. Did we really have a right to spy on this island?

My attention was caught by a disturbance in the water. Time to look to the fishing lures. The frigate birds were also watchful and wheeled over the two lines, taking it in turns to swoop down and pick up the ends in their beaks. In spite of them, Iain managed to hook a barracuda, but, before it could be hauled aboard, the wily fish chewed through the line, taking the hook as a souvenir. I fared better with a skipjack tuna weighing at least fifteen pounds, and we only just had time to slosh the blood off the stern before Iain landed an even bigger yellowfin tuna. We danced about uttering primeval yells of exhilaration. As we crossed the channels leading to the lagoon within the atoll, we felt the tremendous force and turbulence of the ebb tide rushing through the gaps. Two more yellowfin tunas gave themselves up and we became so totally absorbed in the blood and gore that we had to be called back to reality by John, who announced that we were almost at the settlement on West Island. The fish were pushed hastily under cover as we prepared to wrestle with sails and our patent anchor dropper - a plank of wood angled across the bulwarks. Because of doing everything at the last minute it was twice as hectic as usual and a radio call from the yacht Galadriel, already anchored there, put us in more of a turmoil. At last all was ship-shape and we prepared the most delicious meal I can remember - fresh tuna steaks seasoned with salt and black pepper, gently fried. We gorged ourselves and sat back unable to move. The skipper of Galadriel, Willy, found us in that satiated state when he paid us a neighbourly call. He told us that we were only the third yacht to stop at Aldabra in 1983, Galadriel being the second. Intending to stay for two or three days, Willy and his crew had been influenced by the magic of the atoll and had been at anchor for three weeks.

Since the Island Development Corporation had entrusted us with stores for the community on Aldabra, we were not required to pay the landing fee of one hundred rupees per person. The charge was necessarily high but it would have seemed like a fortune to us! John Colly, the warden, motored out to see us and, with the help of his British resident mechanic, Frank, and a Seychellois meteorologist, took the sacks of rice, flour and sugar which had become familiar obstacles in all the cabins. Suddenly we had big open spaces occupied only by a few weevils which got left behind!

We went ashore at dusk and revelled in the unfamiliar luxury of easy chairs in the clubhouse of the Research Station. We watched a perfect sunset against a craggy foreshore, spoke to a sleepy giant tortoise parked on the footpath and hastened back across the reef before too much of it became exposed by the receding water. Truly it was an enchanted land.

Tuesday October 25th dawned in dismal fashion so we used it to put right all the latest things to go wrong. The four tuna fish were likely to become an embarrassment to us because our freezer was only big enough to take one of them. We solved that problem by donating one to the Research Station and by drying another one. Andy took charge of this by cutting the yellowfin into strips and marinading them in a mixture of soy sauce, sugar and salt, a recipe from our Korean friend, Mr Moon. The strips were then threaded onto a line and hung up to dry in the rigging. Some pieces never made it as far as the rigging for we discovered that the texture of the fish had altered during the marinade process and it was quite delicious as it was! The dried strips made a tasty leathery snack to chew on in idle moments.

On the following morning we walked Northwards along the shore of West Island, towards Anse Varre, circling back to the Research Station via one of the areas inhabited by giant tortoises. We spotted only twenty five of the big fellows, for most of the estimated population of one hundred and fifty thousand live on South Island which can only be reached by boat, usually from the lagoon at high water. For most of the year the sea is too rough to allow a voyage and a landing from outside the atoll. It's interesting to note that in comparison there are no more than about ten thousand giant tortoises of a related species on the Galapagos Islands in the Pacific Ocean, the only other place in the world where they live in any great numbers.

Being reptiles with no internal heat regulation system like man's, the tortoises cannot tolerate extremes of temperature. They spend most of the day in the shade of Aldabra's bush, coming out to feed on the open grassy areas mainly in the early morning and late afternoon. If the yearly rains fail, there is a shortage of grass and many tortoises die.

The female lays between one and twenty four eggs in a shallow chamber which she digs in a guano pit. She covers them with soil and then urinates over the nest. This forms a mortar-like mixture which the sun bakes into a hard protective crust over the eggs. This remarkable device keeps predators such as land crabs out of the nest but it also means that baby tortoises cannot get out until the rains soften the soil. The hatchlings can live for a time on the remains of the eggs, but if the rains are late, then the nest becomes a tomb.

Giant tortoises were no strangers to us who had lived four years on Mahe, but it was good to see them roaming freely in complete safety instead of in small pens for the benefit of tourists. I have seen Seychellois girls tickle the shell of a tortoise in a certain spot so as to make him move faster. Children are often photographed having rides on their backs, but here on Aldabra this lumbering beast was king, protected by a small team of people who watched and counted them. Many of the tortoises under regular scrutiny were marked with a thin metal disc embedded in their shell.

The warden joined us for our afternoon exploration of the treacherous surface of the island. In geological terms Aldabra is a recent arrival. Formed by a volcanic cap that grew on top of volcanic mountains, it last emerged from the sea around 80,000 years ago, having been covered by water at least twice before that. This uneven pitted coral forms most of the atoll's surface and is called 'champignon' because of its mushroom-like structure. The weird moonscapes were strangely compelling but it took great concentration not to fall into the cracks and chasms which went down to a depth of two metres in some areas. Several hundred metres from the sea, we came to a salt pool, unique because of its mysterious occupants - the 'upside-down jellyfish'. Instead of having the mantle uppermost with the frilly bits trailing down into the water like any normal self respecting jellyfish, they were floating bottoms up! John lifted one of the pale brown creatures with a stick and turned it over. In slow motion it regained its equilibrium and the position it favoured. So far the mystery has not been solved by scientists to whom Aldabra is a place where nature rules supreme.

We were glad to retreat to the shade of the settlement once more and accepted the invitation to stay for supper - curry goat and baked fish with all the tasty creole trimmings - a sumptuous meal. The shuffling outside the kitchen door indicated the presence of giant robber crabs scavenging for scraps around the dustbins. Knowing them to be powerful enough to dehusk a coconut, steal a cook-

*Our super-catch of four tuna fish along the north coast of
Aldabra.*

A robber crab

*Frigate birds wheel over the mushroom
coral.*

Aldabra is famous for its flightless rails

We stop to look at salt pools in the craggy coral.

ing pot or camera, or amputate a man's finger, I did not rush forward to handle one. I stood back and admired their rich colouring ranging from red/brown to purple, and their menacing claws, from a distance. Inside the clubhouse Willy was tuning his guitar. We joined the crew of Galadriel for a strumming and singing session lively enough to draw the cook from his chores. The wooden hut vibrated with insistent chords, shouted words and tapping feet until all at once we remembered that tides wait for no man. The party came to an abrupt end as we did not want to become shorebound for the night.

Frank Drinkwater, the mechanic, was our guide for our last complete day on Aldabra. He took us East along the North coast in one of the island boats, driven by a powerful diesel outboard. Ever safety conscious, he carried a spare engine and told a grim tale of an islander who, after losing engine power, capsized and was dashed onto the coral. We hung onto the side as we thumped into the waves, the spray threatening to drench our cameras. At last we slipped into the quiet of the lagoon and stopped at Middle Island to entice the flightless white throated rail from the cover of the bushes. After much tapping of shells on stones, which we were assured would attract them, one perky little head emerged, cocked an eye at us and hopped towards us. I waggled my toes like mad because I had heard that waggling toes were irresistible to the flightless rail. My toes obviously weren't as tempting as some varieties, for the ungainly bird turned his back on them. However, a second rail appeared and rewarded my patience by coming close to my outstretched hand with head bobbing in nosy fashion. He soon retreated to the bushes and we left the two of them having a noisy debate on tourism!

The rest of the trip across the North West edge of the lagoon was very special. The mint green water formed a cool backcloth to the mushroom coral. Terns, frigates and boobies filled the air and hovered in our slipstream whilst the mangrove was patched with red where the male frigate birds were puffing out their chests in courtship. These black, almost prehistoric looking birds use the distasteful feeding method of dive bombing other birds, mainly red footed boobies, forcing them to disgorge their catch and then stealing it in mid air. Though sneaky, it provides a thrilling display of aerobatics as the boobies twist and turn to escape their tormentors.

The narrow creeks revealed exotic fish, turtles flippering their way out of our bow wave and rays coasting the floor of the lagoon. Frank talked quietly of sharks he had seen. The heavy beating of wings drew our eyes to a heron rising like a ski jumper from the mangrove. Frank looked at his watch - the reef would be drying - time to return. We left the lagoon and headed for the settlement.

I had spent odd moments in the library of the Research Station, so to round off a perfect day, Lucy joined me for a stroll in the hope of identifying some birds. Happily we recognised turtle doves of a particular Aldabran variety, pied crows, a sacred ibis and a drongo, also special to Aldabra. Pat and Joan walked in the opposite direction and spotted a kestrel. Tiny sunbirds were oblivious of human visitors as they probed the flowers with their long down-curved bill.

Dusk crept over us as Martin's strong arms rowed us back to Christian Bugge. As usual I felt the thrill of possessing such a beautiful vessel as her curves gradually filled my vision. How glad I was that we had brought her back to life, for in some strange way, the pleasure I was deriving from the voyage was insignificant compared with the joy at seeing such an elegant boat ride the waves again. As darkness fell, Pat and I made a tuna curry to repay the hospitality of Frank and John who were joining us for the evening. They were probably tired of fish but the alternative was corned beef, or rabbit droppings in gravy, labelled minced beef. We hoped for more inspired supplies in Durban. Andy and Frank came to an agreement about the Volvo outboard that we wanted to buy for the dory, and also arranged to collect some fendering for same. I think everyone was beginning to notice that I winced and screamed each time the rough edge of the fibreglass dory hit CB's paintwork!

We intended our morning departure from Aldabra to be an impressive one with expert handling of sails and a good turn of speed in the brisk South Easterly wind but we had reckoned without the busy reef beneath us. What John Colly and Frank Drinkwater saw through the viewfinders of their cameras was Christian Bugge drifting along the coast with mainsail flapping and John Hook dangling over the bows in the bosun's chair, hacking ineffectually at a gigantic piece of stag's horn coral latched firmly onto our anchor chain. From our safe position on deck we nagged him to get on with it, but an axe was a puny weapon against such a sea sculpture weighing possibly two hundred pounds. Suddenly it shifted, only to jangle its way down to the very end of the chain. Andy and Martin winched the coral and anchor partnership to the surface and secured a line from the coral to the end of the whisker pole and from there by blocks to the winch. By swinging the pole out over the side and heaving up and down at different angles, they were finally able to trip the coral in the direction which freed it from the chain and sent it plummeting into the depths. We hauled John and the anchor aboard and ignored John's not-very-subtle hints about it being past lunchtime, while we set the sails for close hauling on a port tack. Our next destination was Mayotte in the Comores Islands.

Sagittarius

From Baguettes To Biltong

After an uneventful three day passage we sighted Mayotte and obtained a fix on Isle Pamanzi and Isle M'Zamboro. Mayotte is the only one of the Comores Islands which is inside an encircling reef. It has depths of water up to forty metres and an area up to eight miles wide between the reef and the main island.

We entered through the main passage to the North and enjoyed a gentle sail for twelve miles down through the lagoon to the administrative capital of Dzaoudzi. This is situated on a small island to the west of Mayotte, no more than half a mile across but attached by a causeway to another island, Pamanzi, which has the airport on it. We anchored where we were told, amongst a few other yachts, tidied the decks and prepared to lift the dory over the side. The Port Captain came to see us and told us that the shops and banks would not be open for two days, as it was a public holiday. Trust us! It was not that we were in desperate need of anything in particular, but we had worked ourselves into a state of anticipation for the taste of chocolate. I was also hoping to escape the bread making routine for a few days, but now it looked as if we could do nothing but get on with the chores.

Unlike the other Comores Islands, Mayotte is politically attached to Reunion and is therefore a part of France, boasting a detachment of Foreign Legionnaires and some Naval vessels. Those islands that went their own way, gained independence some years ago, and having been racked by coup and counter-coup are apparently fairly run down now. Although more stable, Mayotte certainly shows no signs of sophistication. The majority of the people are Muslims of East African origin and speak an Arab based language. Many lead a poor existence in flimsy housing, unable to buy the highly priced French goods in small glossy shops. Yet the European influence is strong. Many of the women we saw, were swathed from head to foot in long, flowing sarongs, underneath which they wore Western

Andy, John and Martin prepare the deck for painting in Mayotte.

The 'splodge' technique worked best.

The market at Mamutzu.

Lucy and Joan hide in the long grass as the sun goes down over the crater of an extinct volcano.

style skirts or dresses. Some had daubed their faces with yellow or white paste made from wood pulp in true East African style. A few of the men wore dark suits covered by full length robes. A fez and an umbrella were not unusual finishing touches to an outfit which looked rather cosy for a climate only thirteen degrees South of the equator.

Much tinned and packaged food, normally available in France, was also obtainable in Mayotte but at very high prices. There were displays of cold meat, pate, and sausage, obviously essential to the well being of the Foreign Legion and the French Navy, but out of the question for most of the population. Andy and John eyed the wine which was not overpriced. Perhaps just one bottle.....

On my first visit to the French bakery I took Lucy, Iain and Joan with me. The warm smell drew us to the alleyway where a crowd of people gave us the clue to the bakery entrance. The hot baguettes ran out just before we reached the front of the surge. There was a twenty minute wait before the next batch but this was no chore because there was plenty to see. The portly proprietor chivied the men into action with what sounded like insults and what looked like a cuff round the ear in some cases. The long white rounds of dough were lined up on trays ready to go into the glass fronted oven. Meanwhile a large wad of dough which had been revolving in an electric mixing tub, was lugged by muscular arms and slapped onto a floured table. Lucy's and Joan's eyes widened as the dough was divided and weighed at breakneck speed. They flinched and then grinned as the creamy white substance was hurled about the bakery in casual fashion. A sharp click was audible and we felt the Mahoraise people behind us lean forward as the crusty loaves emerged from the oven and appeared in baskets at our feet. The proprietor revelled in the feeling of power as he ignored the proffered coins and made a great show of getting comfortable. He shuffled through his change and at last told me I could not have the twelve loaves I wanted because bread was "limité", due to a shortage of flour. With our allocation of ten loaves, we hurried back to the boat where hungry mouths and a bubbling coffee pot awaited us.

A spell of settled weather encouraged us to spend a few days on our hands and knees. The sun browned our backs as we crawled around the deck of Christian Bugge, cleaning and priming the pine planks. The top coats were fun. Big brushes and a splodge technique gave a good thick finish and filled all those little cracks which normally invited the rain or salt spray to dance on our dinner. The elastic paint was dry within thirty minutes but needed twenty four hours before it would take the tramp of feet, so we built little bridges and barriers and did half the deck at a time. In the midst of work we spied a small yacht with a Swiss flag making its way towards the anchorage. We were thrilled to see it was a boat called Roi de Soleil which we had known in Seychelles. We had a happy reunion with Gigi and her husband known as Lulu, also their seventeen year old daughter, Anique, who constantly complained good naturedly, that her parents had not been far-sighted enough when they put to sea some seven years ago. She was a child then and fitted her under sized bunk, but now that she had filled out to adult proportions - which Martin never failed to notice - she slept in cramped fashion, rather like Alice in the white rabbit's house after sampling the bottle labelled 'Drink me'.

Lulu was a Swiss baker who had sold up everything for a life at sea. He retained some business interest in Switzerland which necessitated his return for two weeks every October, and this seemed to keep them in funds for the rest of the year. I marvelled at this but never had the sense to find out exactly how he managed it!

As the deck painting progressed, Andy reminded me that there was some lettering to do on the stern of Christian Bugge to show our chosen port of registration. The day I went over the side in the bosun's chair to remedy this, the wind changed from Southerly to Northerly which caused my bottom to be dunked periodically in the waves. I could have done with a four lettered word instead of Southampton! Still, as we motored away in the dory, the result was impressive and could be seen a long way off.

Leaving work behind for the afternoon, we walked up to the rim of an extinct volcano and watched the fruit bats circling over the water in the crater far below us. We played a version of 'hide and seek' called 'forty forty' which sent us all into fits of laughter, more exhausting than the actual running. Joan and Lucy instructed us in the correct playground terminology by yelling "Don't sit on the eggs" to John when he hovered too close to home base. More laughter. Finally we flopped in the grass and watched the sun going down over the shadowy hills beyond the lagoon.

We left Dzaoudzi on November 9th, heading around the South end of Mayotte to take a look at the coast. After spending one night just inside Point

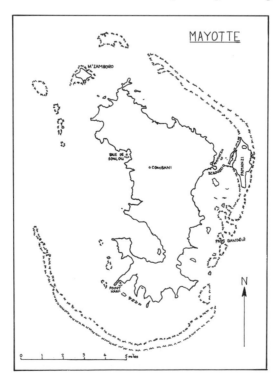

Kani, we sailed on and anchored in Baie de Soulou where there is a small beach and a well known waterfall. Some of us swam and snorkelled while Pat and John walked inland to Combani. The waterfall was a stream, channelled into three powerful jets of water, falling from a height of about twenty feet. The force of it was so great that it actually hurt as it beat on my skin, but it was exhilarating and refreshing. Andy swam lazily round Christian Bugge and suddenly took it into his head to dive down to the rudder. It's just as well that he did, for what he saw caused us to go back to Dzaoudzi the next day and remain there for a further nine days. One of the large pins that holds the rudder in place was missing, and the nut had gone from the other one, thus placing a lot of strain on this remaining pin and on the rudder itself. There was no telling how long it had been like this. Mayotte was not a good place for spares, so all we could do was put our trust in the French Navy. We were not disappointed. A certain Monsieur Pierrot took the project in hand and arranged to have a new rudder pin and two nuts made up in bronze, in spite of yet another public holiday. Meanwhile Saturday November 12th was Iain's fourteenth birthday. He had expected to celebrate it at sea but now it was to be in port. He was deep in a book as usual, oblivious of the whisperings around him. The girls helped me make a fish shaped cake for tea and perfected their entertainment - a dramatisation of 'Little Red Riding Hood' using stick puppets. Good though this was, the real highlight of the afternoon was throwing Iain over the side. He took it calmly, as anyone might in such warm water, but the girls had a giggle over the fact that he was wearing his clothes. Pudding that night was special - Baked Alaska which collapsed because I left it in the oven too long. I suppose it all collapses in the mouth anyway! There were no complaints.

Monsieur Pierrot brought the new rudder pin and nuts and would take no payment. He even declined our invitation to dinner with assurances that he was only too pleased to have helped - truly a gallant Frenchman!

After trailing miles to get our air bottles filled, Andy fitted the pins and we were at last ready to leave Dzaoudzi for the second time, confident that the boat was in tip top condition.

Again we headed South to exit the lagoon through Pass Bandele, a narrow channel that could only be attempted in daylight. Two hours later, with the hills of Mayotte well astern, Andy and John decided to raise the topsail for the first time.

Apart from the fact that three people are needed to cope with the unwieldy topsail yard as it is raised or lowered, there is really no problem, although I would not recommend remaining on the foredeck during this operation unless one is actually involved because it seems likely to lead to decapitation or at the very least, a severe headache. However, I must admit that by the time we reached America, Andy, Martin and John had become quite slick at handling the topsail, and of course there was no doubt that it made us a fine sight. As to whether it made us go faster, the point could be argued either way. Possibly it added half a knot to our speed in some conditions, but the result of the time trials were always clouded by the possibility that the wind had either decreased or increased during the time it took to raise the sail. Regardless of this, we liked to see it gathering that clear wind above the mast, as long as the weather was settled and our course demanded it. Force Two to Three on a beam reach was perfect but if the wind increased to Four it seemed wise to lower it before we felt overpowered.

That first topsail run lasted three clear days and three beautiful nights. Reflected stars danced on the rippled surface of the water and dolphins could be heard snuffling and blowing in the silence, their glittering trails of phosphorescence appearing and disappearing like magic from a wizard's wand.

Iain's and Martin's night watch was disturbed by the noise of a shark attacking a tuna which we had hooked without noticing. The shark got the better half and left us only a small piece of flesh attached to the head. Iain was our chief fisherman and normally trolled with a line either side of the stern. He made his own lures from lengths of red and yellow wool, or tin foil which flashed in the sunlight. Success was erratic, dependent on the area, our speed through the water, and the time of day. The Mozambique Channel proved to be a fertile fishing ground for we caught tuna, barracuda and wahoo on our thirteen day passage from Mayotte to Durban. In a letter to his grandparents, Iain commented that the tuna is a powerful fish, able to dive deep even when towed at six knots. He noted that the wahoo is of the same Scombridae family and has a long retractable fin for very high speeds. We all noted that the flavour and texture of the wahoo is excellent. Barracuda are torpedo shaped fish with menacing teeth, not such good eating as the other two. Now that we had become inveterate scavengers, we were reluctant to reject anything as inedible, much to John's disgust. He disliked all fish and groaned when we were successful, for it meant that he would get an egg with his rice at supper time. Strangely enough the lines often attracted fish during John's watch, and on at least two occasions a flying fish landed in his lap while he was steering! His face showed utter disbelief the day we fried a tiny squid and passed round the morsels at breakfast time. Later, the South Atlantic was to test our determination by yielding up two garfish. They were about a metre in length and rather like an eel with a long flattened head. After picking one over for an hour, I ended up with a big pile of bones and a scanty portion of white flesh.

The journey to Durban was a big hurdle in our minds, with an inhospitable coastline to East and West and the unpredictable weather of the Mozambique Channel. However, as the days went by, our confidence grew, and our daily life took its pattern from the rhythm of the sea. Thirteen days without sight of land was our longest voyage to date and it served as a testing time. As part of a self contained unit, we all had to learn tolerance of each other's foibles which I found hard, since I tended to flare up suddenly if I did not agree with someone else's point of view. Pat was less volatile but struggled with a strong desire to be back on land, which slipped out in the form of little grumbles. Between us we worked things out amicably with particular arrangements for galley duties and the girls' schooling. Pat took care of morning school, usually consisting of maths, English and history from 8.00 - 12.00, while I baked bread and had some time to myself. Whoever was free prepared a simple lunch, after which I usually held some kind of informal schooling such as singing, recorder playing, art and craft or French while Pat had some leisure time. We took it in turns to prepare the evening meal, accepting the fact that it was best for one person to work in the galley at a time. The

Christian Bugge with all plain sail aff the coast of Mayotte.

men had the job of washing up and making coffee after supper. John was normally a calm person with a dry humour, but occasionally he showed fits of moodiness, during which his irritation might bubble to the surface in a stream of quietly uttered comments. Andy made up for me by being excessively calm and controlled in almost every situation. He and John got on well together and both of them devoured numerous books in their spare time. Martin, on the other hand, read little and was happiest when working on an intricate maintenance problem, doing ornamental rope work, or simply gazing at the seascape from the steering position. He acted as a good natured buffer for the girls' teasing and was an adaptable member of the crew.

Iain's main problems were, overcoming his nausea enough to work at his correspondence course, and getting up for night watches. These were usually shared - one person on watch and one dozing but ready to spring into action in an emergency. Pat always woke Martin and Iain as she went off duty. Martin woke Iain a second and third time, shaking his recumbent form and firing threats into his ear. Eventually he arrived at his post as an able watchkeeper but, if he ever took the first half of the watch and slept during the second half, then Andy and I were faced with the problem of making his legs convey him from the pilot berth back to his bunk.

Joan and Lucy were good friends most of the time but, like the adults, had to learn to draw back from conflict in the confined space. Lucy was sometimes moody, retreating to her bunk or a corner of the saloon with an engrossing book. Joan was younger and more restless, with a keen desire not to miss anything that was going on. She did not always appreciate Lucy's inclination to be alone, but this was usually resolved by finding her a job to do in the galley. She loved making cakes, chopping vegetables and mixing salads.

Of course no voyage of the Christian Bugge was complete without its catastrophes. Four days out of Mayotte the mizzen gaff broke by levering round on the aft shroud. While that was under repair, we tore the mainsail in an accidental gybe when the sail hit the runner block. Andy perched on the coach roof with leather palm, needle, thread and scissors to affect the first of many sail repairs on the trip. In a light wind, only half an hour after the main and mizzen were hoist, we broke our mizzen boom. We had lashed it down to the deck from its mid point to prevent the gaff breaking again, but the mizzen caught aback and this was sufficient to snap the boom in half. Later on we resolved the problem by tying the boom forward from its outer end.

We drowned our sorrows in a bottle of wine to celebrate being halfway to Durban.

I think the adult members of the crew were all apprehensive about Durban. For me the thought of fast city life after the quiet islands I had been used to for so long, gave me a sinking feeling in my stomach. I had stored up my own impressions of South Africa, gleaned from stories and news items over the years. Now perhaps I would see for myself. The children were looking forward to bright lights and Christmas treats. In any case, we would have to try the country's dried meat delicacy, biltong.

*Iain takes a close look
at the topsail.*

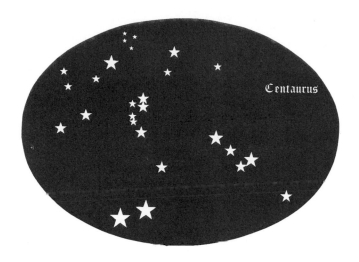

Centaurus

Gales and City Glitter

Getting into Durban turned out to be a complicated business. The wind died away when we still had twenty miles to go. We had to run the engine if we were to get in that night, but this posed a problem of how to keep the engine cool. We had not managed to obtain a new impeller in Mayotte so we were faced with having to find an alternative. We began by connecting up the macerator pump as we had done before, but after a few miles the strain proved too great and it broke down. We rigged an electric bilge pump in its place but, with only three miles to go, that too broke down and we were forced to use a hand pump. The girls did their stint at the hand pump willingly enough, but as soon as the regulation one hundred strokes came to an end, they reappeared on deck to get their first glimpse of the African Continent.

A police launch led us into Durban Harbour and indicated that we were to anchor on the end of a line of yachts. A starched young Immigration Officer hopped aboard with a briefcase full of papers that needed signing, and a very white, long legged young lady checked up on our health. We were just thinking that the reception was efficient and warm, when each of us was handed a bit of paper stating that we were regarded as prohibited persons, not allowed beyond the perimeter of the city unless we paid a deposit of one thousand rand! Luckily we were not thinking of going far. The next blow was that we were all required to report to Immigration at 9.00 a.m. on the following day, December 1st. Staying in bed was obviously not encouraged on the first morning in port.

It was a long walk to Immigration. After the formalities we split up and loitered where our fancies took us. Large department stores and crowded pave-

ments overwhelmed us and made the hours pass quickly. Pat and I arrived back
last with such delights as fresh milk and apples. Pleased with ourselves, we put
down the bags on the quayside and looked for the dory. It did not wholly surprise
us that it wasn't there, for it was quite likely that the others were there before us.
However it gradually dawned on us that the position occupied by Christian Bugge
only three hours before, was now vacant. In its place a strong East wind ruffled the
surface of the water. I rushed backwards and forwards looking for the familiar
wooden masts of Christian Bugge amongst the vast network of rigging. At last I
saw her, far away from the rest, apparently moored to a large green channel buoy
which marked a sand bank. I did not have to wait too long for the answers, because
John appeared in the dory to pick us up.

It seemed that the East wind had been enough to make the anchor drag.
Christian Bugge had accelerated between two small yachts and headed for the
sand bank with her anchor in tow. Miraculously, the anchor chain caught around
the mooring cable of the channel buoy, thus halting her progress in the nick of
time. If the wind had been slightly more Southerly we could have been unlucky
enough to return to more than one wrecked craft.

Andy descended into murky water with an air bottle and felt his way along
the anchor chain to find out the nature of the tangle. Within half an hour we were
able to motor round the cable to free ourselves. We re-anchored, noticing the
anxious looks on the faces of the captains of neighbouring yachts. This time we put
out three anchors to hold us fast in the poor holding ground of Durban Harbour.

The very next day, which dawned windless, was again almost catastrophic for
us. Only Andy and Martin were on board when a South Westerly Buster came
through during the morning. As a South African explained to us later, these winds
come through as if someone has just opened a door! Occasionally the coast is bat-
tered by South Westerlies up to seventy miles an hour. This one was a mere forty
miles an hour but it was sufficient to move Christian Bugge and her three anchors,
this time towards the tug boat basin.

Andy and Martin were below decks working on the hydraulic pump for the
anchor winch, and the first they knew of the disturbance was the judder of the keel
bumping on the sand bank. They rushed on deck, but could do little without the
dory and some extra manpower, especially since the anchor winch was out of action. Luckily Christian Bugge held her new position so there was no immediate
danger.

Meanwhile John was trying to reach the scene in the dory. The outboard had
broken down so he took to the oars. He soon realised the futility of rowing into
such a wind, in spite of the fact that he prided himself on having been an expert
oarsman in his youth! He gave up and clutched at the mooring line of the nearest
yacht and waited until he could be rescued. The harbour ferry boat was still running and the helmsman agreed to take Pat, the children and me to Christian
Bugge. Just as we arrived, Durban Bay Services radioed us with an offer of a place
of safety at their berth in the inner yacht basin. Gratefully we accepted and battled
with the wind and our now hand-operated anchor winch. We motored down the
channel which was only just deep enough for our 9 foot 6 inch draught. Gingerly,

Chritian Bugge dwarfs the other yachts in Durban Harbour.

we felt our way into a berth that was well protected from South Westerly winds by the harbour wall. Perhaps now we could begin to enjoy our stay in Durban!

A new day to day routine evolved. We shopped in little groups, enjoying pre Christmas whispers and giggles about the planned surprises for the festive season. The stores sold absolutely everything, and at prices that were reasonable. Our aim was to stock up with food and head on down to Knysna for the 25th, providing our repairs were completed in time. Bay Services had agreed to let us stay alongside as long as we were waiting for a spare part for our hydraulic pump. Meanwhile we could enjoy our first South African brai (barbecue). It was held under a shelter rigged on the quayside, with the rain sheeting down around us and dripping through the canvas roof. We hugged the fire as we cooked our own sausages and passed round spoonfuls of coleslaw which we had prepared on board. Bay Services provided all the booze and did their best to make it a swinging affair in spite of the weather. Roi de Soleil had come in that morning, so we were able to exchange stories with Gigi, Lulu and Anique once more. We rejoiced at their safe arrival because news of a cyclone had worried us, knowing that they might have been in the affected area. Sadly, the cyclone struck Mayotte and caused considerable damage. In what state were those flimsy houses now I wondered.

Itinerant yachtsmen were lucky enough to be permitted a month's free use of the facilities at Durban Yacht Club. Needless to say, we didn't require a second bidding, and gloried in hot showers every evening. Martin gloried in his fame as a shipwrecked mariner, repeating his story many times to friends he had made on his outward voyage round the coast of South Africa. Since he had no cash, his mournful tale proved a good trade for a drink or two in the bar! The rest of us had no spare money for boozy evenings and we were too large a group to sponge off friends. This left us as usual, making our own entertainment on board, with some memorable exceptions.

Every Sunday evening, the Yacht Club held a family film show when they charged an all-in price for a meal and a film. We decided to combine a pleasurable evening out, with fumigating the boat, thus escaping the toxic smoke and the death throes of those revolting cockroaches, which were observed to be multiplying swiftly in the sticky heat of Durban. We planted the pellets in various parts of the ship, masked all openings, and prepared to disappear for the next four hours. Andy called for everyone to hurry up and grab what they needed before the lighting of the pellets. Slowly, Iain made his way onto the deck, quite oblivious of what was going on, and as the smoke began to billow through all parts of the boat, announced that he had no shoes. "Too bad" yelled Andy, and slammed the door shut. As we approached the stairway to the Yacht Club lounge, we realised that even by bunching together, we could not conceal Iain's enormous feet with their splayed toes. "I'm afraid you can't go up like that sir", rang the voice of the man stationed there for the purpose of inspecting dress. Andy explained our predicament, laying it on about the fumes. After considerable hesitation, the pained voice said, "All right then, but please sit where you will not be noticed". By this time we could hardly contain our laughter, and pushed Iain upstairs where we made him sit with his feet planted right under the table. We even annoyed him by insisting that we fetch his meal for him, thereby preventing him from choosing what he thought was the biggest plateful!

After the film we returned to a lingering acrid smell, but not one dead body. I suspected that the cockroaches were too clever for us. No doubt they would continue to scavenge in the galley, then rush away to their little hidey holes as soon as the lights came on. Recently I had amazed myself by learning to swot the smaller ones with my hand and pick up the bodies, but they could produce babies at a faster rate than I could kill the teenagers. I am glad to say we saw little of the enormous roaches which make that sickening, crunching sound as you step on them.

We managed three more outings during our stay in Durban. The first was to an Ice Show for the girls' benefit (Martin opted out in favour of the Yacht Club bar and Iain went to Jaws 3 in 3-D!), the second to a performance of the Messiah in the impressive City Hall where John embarrassed us by refusing to stand for the Hallelujah Chorus, and the third to a church carol service which was dramatic in presentation with candlelit procession, lighting effects and haunting soloists. All the men opted out of this last expedition but regretted it when we returned with glowing descriptions of the refreshments offered in the church hall afterwards. We emphasised how light the pastry was on the mince pies and how much cream there was on the chocolate cake. As they drooled, we produced some pieces of fruit cake which we had taken from our plates and secreted in our bags at great risk to our integrity as British visitors. At least we had sung lustily at the impromptu carol singing that accompanied the food and the cups of tea.

We were lucky enough to have the use of a small van to do the bulk of our shopping for non perishable goods, which had to last four months. Pat and I staggered to the check-outs trying to steer four large trolleys piled high with tinned goods, sugar, flour etc., the kinds of things which would store well. Brown flour was worth buying because of a government subsidy. Oats and peanut butter were cheap so we went to town on these. We were disappointed that we could not find tinned margarine. This meant we would have to buy fresh margarine and use valuable space in our freezer. Having filled the obvious store cupboards, we began to use the deep cavities formed by the curve of the hull at the back of the galley work tops. Every item was entered in our stores book with a note of its position, a practice which we kept up throughout the voyage. Whoever removed a tin or jar from its storage position was responsible for deleting it from the book.

To stock up with fruit and vegetables, the eight of us trudged one and a half miles to a large covered market where prices were incredibly low. We loaded each other like pack horses, with sacks of potatoes, onions, gem squash, butternuts, cabbages, apples, grapefruit, tomatoes etc. We stored these in net bags slung from the deckhead in the galley and chartroom, where currents of air would help to keep them dry and cool. As well as all this, we decided to try salting some meat in the old tradition, since tinned beef was always expensive and often inferior. Andy

ITEM	QUANTITY	WEIGHT OF EACH	POSITION
BROWN FLOUR		25 KILOS	LARGE TIN, PORT CABIN
CAKE FLOUR		12·5 KILOS	'FLOUR' TIN, DINETTE
BREAD FLOUR		12·5 KILOS	NO 3 TIN, DINETTE
WHITE SUGAR		12·5 KILOS	SMALL TIN, GALLEY
DEMERARA SUGAR		12·5 KILOS	TUB IN MAST CUPBOARD
OATS	5̶4̶ 3̶ 2̶ X	1 KILO	GALLEY CUPBOARD
OATS	5̶4̶ 3̶ 2̶ X	1 KILO	SALOON CUPBOARD
TIN PEACH JAM	5̶ 4̶ 3̶ 2̶ X	900 gm	HEADS CUPBOARD RIGHT
TIN PLUM JAM	4̶ 3̶ 2̶ X	"	" " " MIDDLE
MELON & GINGER JAM	5̶ 4̶ 3̶ 2̶ X	"	" " " MIDDLE
TIN APRICOT JAM	16 15 14 13 12 11 10 9̶ 8̶ 7̶ 6̶ 5̶ 4̶ 3̶ 2̶ X	"	" " " LEFT
PEANUT BUTTER	8̶ 7̶ 6̶ 5̶ 4̶ 3̶ 2̶ X	810 gm	" " BOTTOM
TIN MINCED BEEF	13 12 11 10 9̶ 8̶ 7̶ 6̶ 5̶ 4̶ 3̶ 2̶ +	400 gm	HEADS CAVITY RIGHT
TIN MINCED BEEF	6̶ 5̶ 4̶ 3̶ 2̶ X	400 gm	HEADS CAVITY LEFT

Extract from stores book.

had been reading his ancient copy of Yacht Navigation and Voyaging by Claud Worth, so was well up on what we needed. We consulted a butcher who sold us approximately fifteen pounds of beef topside and fifteen pounds of leg of pork in two to four pound pieces. He also told us where to obtain a specially prepared brine mix containing saltpetre.

According to Worth, a brine solution should be made by dissolving salt in fresh water until a peeled potato just floats in it. An ounce of saltpetre is needed for every four gallons of brine. He advises that a heavy object such as a slab of oak, should be floated on the top of the brine to prevent the meat rising above the surface, for, if any of the fat is exposed to air, it can become tainted, thus spoiling the whole tub. After ten days in the pickle, the meat would be ready for boiling without soaking, but after five weeks it would become saturated with salt and need twenty four hours soaking in several changes of water. From then on it would keep indefinitely without further change.

Andy prepared the tub and put in the pieces of pork and beef. Nothing more was required except to check the brine with a peeled potato again, after the first fortnight, and add more salt accordingly. We intended it for consumption on the long haul from Cape Town to the Caribbean.

We were almost ready to brave the savage sea between Durban and Knysna, miles on down the coast. We attended a meeting at the Yacht Club, at which the speaker was giving advice on the renowned Agulhas Current and on the angry coastline which offered few places of refuge for yachts. We took notes and were duly sobered by tales of gigantic waves, whipped up by strong South Westerlies clashing with the fast moving current. In the event of conditions such as these, we were advised to go inshore and risk a narrow stretch of calmer water, crowded with other vessels doing the same thing.

On December 16th, Andy went through the four to five hour procedure of getting clearance of the port. The sprint began at the Harbour Office and took him to Customs, Immigration, and finally back to the Harbour Office to see the Port Captain. From that moment we had to leave within thirty six hours, or else clear again. In view of reports of a South Westerly on its way up the coast, we were forced to do just that. As the wind began to die without ever reaching gale force, Andy went through all the formalities again and we left our mud berth. That in itself was not easy, for, as the water rose and fell, we had hollowed ourselves a groove in the mud. A motor boat took pity on us and towed us into the channel. We headed out of the harbour, knowing that there was no sanctuary before East London.

We need not have worried, for we had little chance of stopping. After a few hours of calm weather, during which we motored in search of the Agulhas Current (local yachtsmen test the water with a thermometer for a significant rise in temperature) to carry us Southwards, we were hit by a North Easterly gale. We shot down the coast like a bat out of hell. We reefed the main and kept an eye on the tell tales, enjoying the exhilaration of speed. Reports came through on the radio, of expected South Westerlies, which prepared us for the possibility that we might have to take refuge in East London. Suddenly the Force 7 died away to nothing and we began to put up full sail in order to move at all. As we worked on deck, East London radioed an urgent message that a South Westerly Force 9 was with them at the moment. We looked at the horizon, now shelved by an ominous line of cloud. Yes, we could see it moving towards us. We could not afford to be caught with so much sail up. Hastily we took three reefs in the main, two in the staysail, and removed the jib altogether. Wham! A gust struck hard and pushed us over for a full five seconds, but as we righted we realised that the wind was already fading again. Before long we were motoring into East London in a flat calm. We had completed 190 miles in thirty two hours - good going for an old gaffer!

Christian Bugge gets into the groove as we leave port.

Unscheduled Operation

Our stay in East London was as brief as officialdom would permit. No wonder some yachts leave without saying goodbye! Our skippers did not want any possibility of problems at our next port of call, so we endured the bureaucratic procedure which kept us until noon of the next day, December 21st.

We left with a light East wind which gradually increased and became more Northerly, until during the night, the watchkeeper's inattention permitted a gybe. A gaping hole appeared in the mainsail as the boom swung over and clobbered the runner. This was not the kind of tear that Andy could deal with from the coachroof. Our vision of Christmas in Knysna began to recede and we scrutinised the charts to consider the chances of motor sailing into Port Elizabeth, where we would be more likely to get a good sail repair. It was worth a try. Having allowed ourselves to be whisked far out from the coast, we now had to struggle across the current to get back in. Andy and John passed the time by removing the mainsail from the boom and bagging it, a mammoth task in itself. As the day wore on, the wind changed to our advantage, enabling us to enter Port Elizabeth eighty miles and seventeen hours after the accidental gybe.

We moored alongside the tug wharf, close to the Algoa Bay Yacht Club. Immediately, friendly tug men materialised to offer advice and help. We had barely finished securing our warps and placing tyres along our length to protect Christian Bugge from the wall, before we were told that there was a chance of us being connected to shore power via the pilot boat. What a joy that would be, not to have to run our unsociable generator. Andy fostered the friendship with the tug men.

Just ahead of us we could see the familiar lines of a boat called Sea Shanty which had sailed into the Seychelles in November 1982 after voyaging from Port Elizabeth, up through the middle of the Atlantic to the Mediterranean, where they spent several years working their way across to the East end and the Suez Canal. They had to sail non stop from Suez to Seychelles because of the inhospitality of the Red Sea ports. We had come to know the owners, Sue and Dave Sanderson, quite well, for they had stayed several months, glad to rest up in a place that did not harass South African yachtsmen. They were delighted to see Christian

Bugge in Port Elizabeth and came aboard with a bottle of wine. They were still living on Sea Shanty, but were in the process of selling her with a view to buying something bigger. In their anxiety, Sue's children, who were quite grown up with families of their own, gently mocked their parents for their nomadic and irresponsible retirement. Personally I admired their exploits and hope I will have as much energy when I reach that stage in my life.

We accepted the fact that we were to spend Christmas against a dirty wall with a view of other dirty walls, a handful of yachts, port cranes and the untidy paraphernalia of the docks. At least we did not need to unload the dory, and the shops were but a step or two from the entrance to the docks. Inevitably we thought of last minute purchases to make before the 25th. Sue and Dave assisted with their car whenever possible and delighted the children by fetching a genuine Christmas tree which we fastened to the main mast on deck. Joan and Lucy did not care where we spent Christmas as long as we were stationary. They had been adamant that, even if we were in mid ocean when the day arrived, we were to drop anchor! Well, they had what they wanted. Excitement mounted. Martin took it upon himself to fasten our signal flags in the official order so that we could make our mark on Port Elizabeth by dressing overall. I made our own personal house flag, incorporating the symbol of the Norwegian Rescue Service with our number, RS41. This was flown from the top of the mizzen, whilst the Red Ensign was flown from the main mast.

The day came. The girls were up at 5.00a.m. to open their stockings full of sweet and savoury treats. Iain opened his more nonchalantly, not wanting to be a child and yet reluctant to miss out on childish things. Around mid morning, after Pat, John and Joan had been to church on behalf of the whole crew, the eight of us gathered in the saloon to give each other little presents, many of them homemade. Lucy had made me a spectacles case, with HELEN embroidered on the outside in big letters. She had also stitched a small traycloth in secret moments. Pat and John produced enamelled mugs for all, with hand painted Christian Bugges on the side. Martin delighted Lucy and Joan with a cheesecloth blouse for each of them. I was touched by his thoughtfulness, especially in view of the fact that he was broke! We were all glad that he had made the decision to stay with us, at least as far as Cape Town.

The turkey was succulent. Lucy recorded the whole meal in her diary - turkey, bread sauce, stuffing, peas, carrots, sausage, bacon, gravy and sadly, boiled potatoes instead of roast. Although the oven on our Shipmate stove was a good size, it could not cope with roast potatoes as well as the bird and all its trimmings. Pat was responsible for the Christmas pudding with the help of her culinary bible, Mrs Beeton's Cook Book, and a very good pudding it was too. Pink with wine, we set off for a brisk walk to St. George's Park to pick up an appetite for cake and mince pies!

Boxing Day brought the first of a succession of newspaper reporters searching for scraps of news in the void of the Christmas holiday. Headline - 'New life for a tough old sea dog' in the Eastern Province Herald. Next came a woman who wanted to write a piece about the difficulties of cooking Christmas dinner aboard.

New life for a tough old sea dog

On board the coverted Norwegian rescue ship, the Christian Bugge, on its way from the Seychelles to England, via Africa, the Americas and the Azores, are (back row from left) Pat Hook, Martin Shaw, John Hook, Andrew Smallwood and Ian Smallwood, and (front from left) Helen Smallwood, Joan Hook and Lucy Smallwood.

HERALD REPORTER
A CONVERTED Norwegian rescue vessel, built in 1935, arrived in Port Elizabeth on Christmas Eve on its way to Britain from the Seychelles via South Africa, the Americas and the Azores.

The vessel, once destined to see out its days

Ex-rescue vessel, fishing boat. is now under sail

Newspaper cutting from Eastern Province Herald, Tuesday December 27th 1983.

Pat and I answered with tongue in cheek and laughed over the resulting article. We were described as '....usually economical eaters' who had decided to '....splurge' this Christmas. A similar article appeared in the Evening Post the next day and we began to wish that the reporters would leave us alone, but they were not the only people in Port Elizabeth to show an interest in us. Every day, people of all ages and walks of life, wandered along the tug wharf and paused to look. From the saloon windows we saw only the legs as they halted and shuffled backwards and forwards to give the spectator a better view. Sometimes they would bend down and look in. This would embarrass them because we were looking out. If Andy went to work on deck you could be sure that he would spend two thirds of the time chatting to bystanders, and occasionally he would offer to show complete strangers round the boat, regardless of what activities were going on down below! He had extreme patience and tolerance for nosy parkers in general and was impressed by the knowledge and friendliness of those in Port Elizabeth.

A jolly lady called Dot was also interested in Christian Bugge, and it was she who repaired our mainsail with a heavy duty sewing machine. Again Dave's car came in very useful for transporting the sail to and from her home, but there was one car journey we did not expect to have to make.........

Having celebrated New Year in company with a few other yachties, we made preparations for leaving Port Elizabeth on Wednesday January 4th. Generally speaking, we were becoming ﾚed to delays and last minute changes of plan, but it did come as a shock to me to find myself being wheeled into an operating theatre at 11.00a.m. on Tuesday 3rd. It all happened so quickly. I awoke at 3.30a.m. with a pain which I did not recognise. It niggled away at my inside until it settled on the right side of my abdomen. I couldn't sleep and felt slightly feverish, until at 4.30 I left my bunk to fetch the 'Ship Captain's Medical Guide', twentieth edition, published by Her Majesty's Stationery Office. On page 171, I found a list of abdominal pains and followed the columns across to 'probable causes'. I took my pulse which proved to be erratic and on the high side. Having diagnosed my condition, I went back to bed as there did not seem to be much point in panicking - after all, surely an appendicitis had a slow build up. I tossed and turned so much that Andy became wide awake and left his bunk. He returned with the Medical Guide and the same conclusion as me. The pain intensified. Perhaps we should take some action. Andy went round to Sea Shanty and found Dave shaving in the early morning sun. I tip toed past the sleeping girls and called softly to Pat that I was just going to hospital with an appendicitis, but it would probably turn out to be chronic wind. I was desperately trying to persuade myself of this as I spoke. I entered the hospital just after 6.00 and was wheeled on a trolley into a small room, where I was told to wait for a doctor. Andy sat beside me. I worried about the cost of hospital treatment and whether we could get it back on our medical insurance. Andy was outwardly calm and confident as usual. A succession of white coated men and women visited me, examined me and asked me endless questions. By 9.00a.m. their diagnosis tal-

Andy and Martin relaxing after unaccustomed eating and drinking.

A real tree gave the ship a festive air.

lied with mine made at 4.30 and I knew that a Mr Waterworth was going to operate quite soon. Waves of pain which made me feel limp and disorientated, were
helped by an injection before I was wheeled along a maze of corridors to a ward,
high up in the building. I was undressed and presented with more questions and
forms to sign, barely finished when the porter came to push me to theatre. By this
time I did not really care about anything and, through the mist, was just aware of
Andy touching my hand and waving goodbye.

Sometime later, I opened my eyes to take in the beds around me, the bustling nurses and the drip connected to my hand. I drifted into a dream world again
until just before visiting time, when I made the effort to prop up my body to receive guests. Andy and Lucy had managed to get a lift to the hospital and had
brought the traditional grapes which they now proceeded to nibble since I was
only allowed liquids. Iain sent his personal cassette player and a selection of tapes
to keep me entertained. He promised to visit me the following day. Andy and Lucy
were likely to have to walk the three miles back to Christian Bugge that night. I
was not very appreciative of their efforts for I just longed to go back to sleep.

Next day, I talked to other patients in the ward, many of them appendix cases
like myself. It seemed that I was one of the more dramatic examples. All those I
spoke to, had had grumbling pains for days or weeks before the operation. This set
me thinking about what might have happened. Supposing we had been far out to
sea. What then? When the surgeon made his round of the ward , I put the question
to him. Without hesitation he replied, "You would have been a goner". Apparently my appendix had turned gangrenous very quickly, and if I had not had the operation promptly, peritonitis would have occurred. I came out in a cold sweat as I
imagined the scene - my family grouped around me, not knowing how to cope. I
saw Andy wondering whether to attempt an operation with the kitchen knife while
the boat rolled in a boiling sea. They would have had the horror of it all, for I
would have been beyond reason. What a narrow escape they had had, and how
grateful I was that circumstances had brought us to Port Elizabeth for such an
emergency. Thoughtfully, I drank bowls of soup and cups of tea.

One of the auxiliary nurses was quite an entertainer. She could be heard several wards away, telling crude jokes, most of which I missed because she spoke in
Afrikaans. I knew the stories were blue from the reactions of the patients and the
'nudge nudge, wink wink' expressions on her face. The other patients made an effort to talk English to me at times and many of them had seen the photographs in
the local press. I heard quite a lot about National Service from one lady whose son
had just done his two years, but was still having to report for duty for a few weeks
each year. All the patients, nurses and doctors were white. The only black face I
saw was that of the cleaner, who shuffled round sullenly while one particular nurse
ordered her around in a most unpleasant manner. I was told that the 'blacks' had
their own hospital up the road. There were some sidelong glances the day Joan
came to visit me!

While I suffered the agonies of trying to walk with a very sore tummy and a
drip hooked up onto a mobile pole, (actually I had a jolly good rest in hospital and
enjoyed myself enormously) the resourceful crew of the Christian Bugge took ad-

vantage of the delay and decided to slip our home for her routine antifouling which was due every six months or so. This meant that, when I was discharged on the fourth day, I faced a six metre high ladder and the prospect of a two hundred metre walk to the Yacht Club every time I needed the loo! I suppose that's really why I recovered so quickly.

Slowly I climbed the ladder and was escorted by excited girls to the saloon where a 'Welcome Home' cake awaited me. Lucy and Joan giggled as they pointed to a gruesome imitation of my appendix in melted chocolate. It tasted good. I was cosseted for a full twenty four hours while everyone got used to me being around again, and then happily, they left me to do whatever I felt capable of attempting.

My recovery was not so quick that I could get involved in the cleaning and antifouling of the hull. I cheered the spattered workers from the sidelines every time I did the long shuffle to the Yacht Club. Since no serious worm damage was discovered, we entered the water with a smart bottom after only four days. Through numerous phonecalls, Andy had ascertained that Port Elizabeth had one of the few slips on the East coast of South Africa which was able to take our draught. Consequently, we had to resign ourselves to a heavy bill of five hundred rand.

With the two old crocks patched and well, there was nothing to prevent us leaving. Sue and Dave came round for a farewell supper and were treated to an entertainment which the girls had been rehearsing all day. A worn tape of a piece by Mozart rasped the night as Lucy and Joan danced on deck, resplendent in bikinis and tinsel. I thought it was a delightful show, particularly since they had choreographed it all themselves. As I watched them gaining confidence from each other, I knew it was one of those moments which I wanted to capture and treasure for years to come. On the final curtsy, the spell was broken and they dissolved into giggles of embarrassment.

During our very last day, we squeezed in a trip to the Fire Station, organised by Sue's son-in-law who was the Chief Fire Officer in Port Elizabeth. Being almost man-sized, Iain obligingly dressed up in the various protective suits for some photographs. The girls tried on hats and sat in the very latest fire engine. I resisted the opportunity to slide down the pole as I did not fancy the idea of having my scar restitched.

Just before we set sail that evening, we received a copy of the latest Evening Post containing yet another story about us. Headline - 'Crew member misses op at sea by a day' and a jolly picture of eight faces smiling goodbye to Port Elizabeth. We cast off warps at 2225 hours, hustled by John who was adamant in his superstition that we should not leave on the following day, Friday January 13th.

Triangulum
Australis

Knysna

The wild East coast of South Africa cherishes its one natural harbour at Knysna. The enclosed sandy lagoon is so sheltered that to enter from the open sea is like opening a door into another world. The narrow entrance is between two rocky headlands, bridged by a bar which wise yachtsmen cross only at or near high water. In days gone by, square riggers used to come and go through the Heads, risking the undertow and concealed rocks to ship hardwoods such as blackwood, yellow-wood and stinkwood from the little port. Now the long established sawmill deals mostly in pine and the protected waters provide leisure pursuits for South Africans with a healthy bank balance. Many holiday makers tour the lagoon in ostentatious motor boats with little consideration for sailing vessels and little knowledge of the effect of wind and tide. Those who are not well off enough to own a boat, hire one of the floating caravans (aptly nicknamed because of their shape) for a day and drive round and round other boats before 'pulling up' (many had no idea of correct anchoring procedures!) at one of the small sandy beaches within the lagoon.

Inevitably, stories revolve around Knysna Heads - stories of daring and drunkenness. We heard of sailors who made a habit of shooting the bar in rough conditions or at low water, just to gain glory in the Yacht Club afterwards. Folklore told of one motor boat which had slammed into a large wave and catapulted its occupants into the water, where they were whirled onto the rocks. Many visitors to Knysna spend hours at the Heads watching the capricious waves dance across the bar. At high water they have the added thrill of seeing boats whisked in on the surf, trying to stay in control. A visiting yacht is sometimes forced to extend its stay by many days because the Heads are impassable.

At 0900 hours on January 14th, Christian Bugge was one of two boats waiting to attempt passage of the Heads. We had made good speed from Port Elizabeth and had been forced to 'heave to' for much of the night. Now we waited for high water in company with a Brazilian yacht called Vagobundo. We hailed each other with compliments and, to pass the time, arranged to hoist full sail so that Vagobundo could take a picture of our topsail, as yet unphotographed.

We scurried about the deck to prepare the sheets while Christian Bugge kept a steady course under staysail and mizzen, making one and a half knots. Both boats were on starboard tack, Vagobundo to weather of Christian Bugge. I was below deck when an ominous thud resounded through our hull. It was followed by a scraping sound, as if something was sawing at our timbers. I threw myself up on deck expecting all manner of catastrophes. At first I thought Vagobundo was impaled upon our bowsprit, but a second look made me realise that we towered over her too much for that. Instead we were locked together, still making way, with our bowsprit between Vagobundo's mainsail and backstay. Our bobstay chain was sawing at her toerail with the up and down movement of the waves. The skipper gazed in horror and disbelief at the giant above him. For seconds we too stood transfixed like a waxwork tableau. Then we leapt in all directions to lower sail and start the engine. With care we reversed off the yacht whose light modern construction seemed so vulnerable next to our massive timbers. Vagobundo retired to lick her wounds and we held an inquest.

True, no one had actually been holding Christian Bugge's steering wheel when the collision occurred, but we had been maintaining a steady course on starboard, with trimmed staysail and mizzen. It appeared that Vagobundo's skipper had drawn ahead of us, gybed round across our bow and misjudged his position. His boat still appeared to be seaworthy, but we remained tense and ready to offer assistance if necessary. Cautiously Vagobundo approached. The skipper managed a sheepish smile and apologised more by hand movements and facial expressions

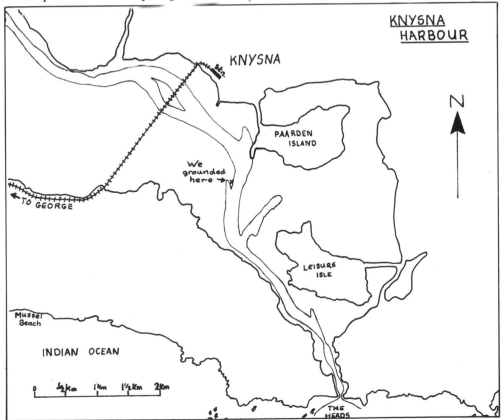

than by words. He assured us that he had sustained damage only to his toerail, stanchion and pushpit. We breathed a sigh of relief and thought how lucky he was. Somewhat deflated, we turned our thoughts to Knysna Heads once more. An hour before high water, John radioed Knysna base for information about the swell. We were told that conditions were not favourable but that we should wait until high water because of the ever changing situation. Martin pointed to Vagobundo, now a dot moving steadily on down the coast. Obviously the skipper had had enough excitement for one day.

At high water John radioed a second time and heard that conditions were still doubtful. Was it essential that we come in now, we were asked. Put like that the answer had to be no, but on the other hand we were anxious to meet up with some friends whose bicycles we were transporting from Durban. Apart from this we were looking forward to calling somewhere with clean air, for Christian Bugge was now a very dirty grey ship after the steam train smuts of Port Elizabeth docks. A final guarded piece of advice was forthcoming. "Entry may be made with care". We decided to go in close under engine and gauge the intervals between waves. As we hovered, our engine went dead. Luckily it was just a question of switching to the other fuel tank, but it could have been most inconvenient if it had happened a few minutes later. The waves appeared to be breaking every six minutes. The consensus of opinion was that we should go for it!

We waited for a wave to break and followed it in. A rush of water accompanied us. Rocks loomed on either side. The helmsman gripped the wheel and tried to stick to the recommended course. Suddenly a rogue wave materialised, lifting and thrusting us forward on the outer bar. We slewed round in a partial broach but regained our heading without difficulty and after the momentary panic we enjoyed an exhilarating ride. Daring to look behind at the white water I found myself thinking, "There's no going back now"! Within moments we were in calm water and the steep cliffs were opening out to reveal a serene lagoon flanked by gentle slopes. Off came the sea going sweaters as we hugged the port side where the channel was deepest. John radioed Knysna base to thank them for their help and to tell them we had achieved entry without mishap. Unwisely he added, "We'll try not to go aground on your sandbanks!"

Either we did not follow the markers accurately enough, or there was an uncharted sand spit protruding into the channel. We prefer to believe the latter but whichever way you look at it, it was an humiliating start to our stay in Knysna. Why oh why did John have to make that remark! There we were making our grand approach to the yacht club anchorage when suddenly we weren't going anywhere any more. A dinghy full of laughing faces - friends from Seychelles and more recently Durban - arrived on the scene to welcome us and commiserate. They tossed us mail which had been redirected from Port Elizabeth, then climbed aboard to pool their ideas with ours for shifting our sand berthed old lady. Having entered Knysna at high water, it was likely that we were fighting a falling tide, in which case every second counted. We raised sail for the wind to blow her off. We put out an anchor and ran a line from it back to the main mast to haul her over on her side. We motored forwards, backwards, fast and slow and all it proved was that we were

Well and truly aground in Knysna Lagoon.

well and truly stuck. Gradually activity ceased and someone put the kettle on. I pulled out the letter from Andy's father. Lo and behold, in his first paragraph he warned us about going aground in Knysna!

I smiled to myself as I thought of my father-in-law's involvement in our project. He was with us in spirit throughout the trip until tragically, he died in May just as we reached Trinidad. A sailing man all his life, he appreciated the magnitude of our adventure and lived it with us through books, maps and letters. He offered advice, anecdotes and hints about the ports ahead of us although he had never travelled abroad himself to any great extent. We did not always heed his advice but his letters were sorely missed after Trinidad. Now I looked at the close handwriting and wondered if his words could have prevented our latest predicament if they had arrived in time.

Slowly the water receded and Christian Bugge heeled over on her port side. Pat and I edged our way along the dinette with our bottoms pinned to the downward side. We prepared the evening meal under difficulties, having to haul ourselves uphill to the galley cupboards and cooker. It seemed strange to be tipped up and yet so still.

We had to wait twenty four hours for a tide that was high enough to allow us back into the centre of the channel but at last Christian Bugge was able to anchor in honourable fashion. There we stayed for five whole weeks, delayed by the need for new parts for the dog clutch drive which connects the hydraulic pump to the front of the engine. These had to be obtained from various sources that were not the most efficient of organisations. We used the time to spruce ourselves up with fresh paint on the topsides and some varnish above and below decks. There was always plenty of work to be done.

We declined the hospitality of the Knysna Yacht Club, mainly because of their charges. These were understandably much higher than those of the ports we had stopped at previously but we considered them too high for the very basic facilities and for our dwindling coffers. Thus we anchored well out, used a public landing stage for our dory, and showered on board. Martin wangled honorary membership of the Yacht Club on the strength of his sad story!

Each week we took time off for outings. One particular trip was made possible by 'Happy', a middle aged man with a warm and generous nature. After

An aerial view of the entrance to Knysna Lagoon.

The ostrich soon found out how to unseat his new rider.

only two chance meetings he offered to take Joan, Lucy, Iain, Andy and me in his car to the Safari Ostrich Farm. It was good to get out to see some of the scenery of South Africa although part of our route lay through the arid area known as the Little Karoo. At the Ostrich Farm we learned about the characteristics of these strange flightless birds. Joan and Lucy stood on some eggs to demonstrate the strength of the shell. They were told about the tremendous power of the ostrich's legs and about its stamina, which enables it to run at thirty kilometres per hour for ten hours at a stretch, if necessary. They sat aside a penned ostrich for the usual photographs and looked at the grand estate house known as a 'feather palace'. The highlight of the visit was when invitations were issued to volunteer riders. Andy was pushed forward and climbed meekly onto the wary bird. The ostrich lulled him for a moment or two by doing nothing, then suddenly shot forward a few steps and jammed on its brakes. Andy was catapulted over its head, much to the amusement of the spectators. Not being able to afford a feather boa, we left the souvenir shop with a small piece of ostrich biltong!

Happy drove on to the Cango caves at Oudtshoorn. Here we enjoyed dank passages and stalactites which had been around far too long to even think about. Vast caverns opened up in front of us and were lit like magic by coloured lights to show a ballerina, witch, waterfall, madonna........Someone's imagination knew no bounds. I had a stiff neck and began to long for sun light. Iain, Lucy and Andy wanted to do the optional extra which meant crawling and wriggling their way through the narrow passages and orifices of the final section of the caves. Happy excused himself on account of his age. Joan quaked visibly and clutched my hand so the three of us waved goodbye to the intrepid explorers and retraced our steps to the exit for cowards. Half an hour later we all met up again in the souvenir/refreshment room, Lucy's eyes shining with excitement over the memory of that creepy place.

Our trip to George was not quite so carefree. While it left us all with a bitter after taste, its effect on Joan was far more devastating. As black among whites, Joan had so far been cushioned against prejudice. As a small child, brought up in North Wales, she had received special consideration and attention because of her cute looks. In Seychelles, she had been accepted in the way that all colours of skin are accepted there. Often mistaken for a Seychellois girl, she intrigued local people when they discovered she was West Indian - again special consideration and smiling interest. John and Pat were very protective, always watchful for any difficult situations which might arise. I suppose we could not expect to remain in South Africa for any length of time without coming up against apartheid, but I don't think we were really mentally prepared for the actuality.

In Durban and Port Elizabeth we had felt the rumblings as from a distant volcano. Strolling in a group, with Joan and Lucy holding hands and laughing together, we had become conscious of turned heads and curious looks because, although blacks and whites mingled in the city, they rarely walked together. Outwardly, Durban appeared enlightened. Few signs remained in the shopping areas but beaches were segregated and beggars always black. In the jostling central market where we stocked up with cheap fruit and vegetables, we saw few faces as pale as ours. We were so conspicuous that, as I turned down an alleyway to go to a lady's lavatory, a white man in a neat suit pounced on me and told me it would be better to use the one in his office just down the road. He was so insistent that I followed meekly and did as I was told. Brief conversations with Asians in shops and market stalls indicated that, although discriminative notices were no longer in evidence, the barriers still existed, as insurmountable as ever.

Water was always a trouble spot. Pat decided that white South Africans were afraid that colour came off in water. At a paddling pool in Durban, she had to explain that Joan was a British visitor to the country and as such was entitled to swim alongside white children. This was accepted by the attendant but attracted disapproving glances from other mothers. After a similar incident at a water chute on the beach of Port Elizabeth, Pat always carried Joan's passport, alert to the need to smooth things over as quickly as possible in the event of a challenge. Lucy helped by sticking to Joan like glue and being ready with a quick answer. In a Port Elizabeth changing room, two girls commented jeeringly that it was for Europeans only! Lucy shot back with, "She's more European than you!" and the moment passed.

Somehow Joan was steered through awkward situations without her becoming completely aware of the cause. Knysna Railway Station changed all that.

We were there at 8.00a.m. to buy a return ticket entitling us to take the bus to George and the steam train back to Knysna via the scenic route, the main reason for the journey. Martin elected to stay behind, so the seven of us crowded into the Ticket Office. We paid our money and took the tickets without looking at them. As we stood waiting for the bus, Pat glanced at the sheaf of papers. One was different, a third class ticket. Silently, with the light of battle in her eyes, Pat strode back towards the ticket office. She was gone a long time. Every minute made us more uneasy, prepared to take a united stand and ask for our money back if necessary. The bus arrived and so did Pat, trembling with the effort of self control. Quietly she murmured, "It's all right, we can go". Then she told us what had happened. She had had to grapple with the inflexible nature of the Afrikaaner in the ticket office who could not or would not understand that Joan was a member of the family, and as such could travel with us. As far as he was concerned the rules said that blacks and coloureds travelled in the back of the bus and whites in the front. "Lady, this isn't an international service you know". Pat pointed out that Joan was a British visitor and only nine years old. "So what?" She offered to go third class with Joan. "Not allowed lady". Pat played her trump card. She threatened to contact the Minister of Transport. He flinched. Well, perhaps something could be done, but the bus driver would have to be asked whether he would mind and it would also have to be cleared with other first class passengers. This was something of a joke because there were only eight first class seats and we would have seven of them!

We boarded the front of the bus while the bus driver chatted amiably with glances in our direction. We seemed to have gained some kind of notoriety. Those whose skin colour matched Joan's, crowded to the rear entrance with numerous boxes and bags. The solid partition prevented any further communication between front and back. Joan cuddled up to her dad for reassurance, no longer the naive little girl of yesterday. From that day on, if an outing was planned for the crew of Christian Bugge, Joan would ask, "Am I allowed there as well?"

The journey to George was through quiet villages and pleasant scenery, but the picture in my mind is of a narrow, dusty stretch of road where the bus had a scheduled stop. Not content with separate seating arrangements, the system decreed that white people should buy their tickets when safely aboard the bus and black people from the driver's window. And so it is that I see an old, old man shuffling slowly down the middle of the road to buy his ticket. The sudden knowledge of that old man's degradation struck me in the pit of my stomach and between my eyes. I felt ashamed to be there in my first class seat, ashamed to be white, ashamed to be part of a world that allowed such things. I wanted to leap up and do something - but what? The old man certainly wouldn't thank me for a scene.

We trundled on to George, walked round the town and caught the steam train back to Knysna.

Equally disturbing, but with a touch of humour, was an incident at the Knysna open air swimming pool. It was a small pool, close to the sea shore and little used while we were there because local children were in school. Pat took the girls one afternoon. There was no admission charge and the black attendant watched the three of them go into the deserted changing rooms. Only when they reappeared in costumes did he approach Pat with, "Sorry lady, this pool is for white children." Pat trotted out her usual speech which prompted, "No lady, you don't understand. This pool is for white children only." Out came the passport and back he came apologetically, "Sorry lady, the rules say only white children can swim here." Pat was perplexed but dogged. "She *is* white" said she firmly, surprised at her own words, but even more surprised at his reply, "OK. lady, go on in".

Roi de Soleil appeared one day in company with an Australian yacht called Sandpiper. This was a good excuse for an expedition to the mussel beach. I have never seen a cove so black with mussel shells. We darted in all directions, claiming

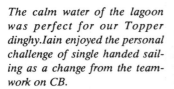

The calm water of the lagoon was perfect for our Topper dinghy.Iain enjoyed the personal challenge of single handed sailing as a change from the teamwork on CB.

to have found the most gigantic ones on our particular rock. Those who wanted a break from prizing the shells from their perch, collected firewood. Before long the first pot was bubbling and we were able to sample the fare - the freshest, most flavoursome mussels I am ever likely to eat. At the water's edge, Lulu spotted a pair of octopuses in a rock pool and immediately ducked down and seized first one and then the other. Anique was delegated to 'hoodwink' the creatures by getting rid of their ink sacs and turning their hoods inside out to render them helpless. Two would make a good curry I thought to myself, but three would be even better, so, armed with a stick, I wandered off alone to the deeper rock pools where I soon spied an unsuspecting octopus in a crevice. Determined to conquer my fear of its eight writhing tentacles, I forced myself to thrust out an arm and clutch the gelatinous mass. Once he realised that I had him, he wrapped his arms around mine. This made me fling him away onto the sand. I found some more courage and picked him up again, ran a few steps and threw him down as I felt the clammy touch of his suckers. In this way I returned more or less triumphantly to the mussel party. However, I did not get the hero's welcome I thought I deserved - after all, only five weeks ago I had been in hospital for an appendectomy and now here I was battling with an eight legged monster!

A notice on the beach made it quite clear that we were only allowed to take away twenty five mussels per person. Since we assumed that those already consumed were not to be counted, we set about checking the numbers that remained and making them up accordingly. I believe there were fourteen of us, entitling us to three hundred and fifty of those giants. We climbed the steep cliff path with our treasure and headed back across the ridge to Knysna lagoon. That evening our friends congregated aboard Christian Bugge for octopus curry and a variety of mussel dishes fit for a king.

Towards the end of our stay in Knysna, an impetuous run along a rickety pontoon brought Andy to his knees with a sprained ankle and put him out of action for 'Die Olifant Wandelpad'(The Elephant Walk) in the forest around Diepwalle. He and Martin prepared a barbecue while the rest of us slogged round the course in blazing sun. Actually only Pat, John and Iain did the full eighteen kilometres. Joan, Lucy and I did a shortened circuit which we improved upon by missing a turning and becoming lost! After finding no trace of elephant's dung, let alone an elephant, we all managed to meet up at the appointed nosh area where we talked of blisters and imagined trumpetings. It was good to get into the soft green of the hills after the vivid blue of the sea.

In between the outings, we gave Christian Bugge the most thorough face lift she had had since the start of the voyage. We repainted the topsides completely, in spite of local curiosity which brought boat loads of day trippers speeding close in to our anchorage to send breaking waves over our fresh and tacky gloss. Fist shaking and shouted abuse had little effect. We simply had to resign ourselves to getting up early to miss the rush and posting a watch so that, at the crucial moment we could at least preserve our balance along with the paint tin.

The air was balmy. In both work and play we found relaxation. We wind-surfed, explored creeks in the dory and topper dinghy, made fleeting friendships, and at last, on February 21st we said our goodbyes to Knysna - a day later than Roi de Soleil and Sandpiper. The water at the Heads was not as calm as it first appeared for a breaking wave took us by surprise and caused an unstowed five gallon water container to burst as it crashed to the floor of the dinette.

White water takes us through the Heads.

Cape of Storms

The Southernmost point of the African Continent was our next hurdle. All we had to do was touch latitude 35° South and then we could head for Cape Town. The thought of negotiating the notorious Cape of Storms was pushed well to the back of our minds as we concentrated on careful navigation and the recording of weather forecasts.

After twelve hours of strengthening South Easterlies, we had progressed past Mossel Bay and had taken bearings on Cape St Blaize and Ystervark Point. Then, during daylight hours of February 22nd the wind died right away, swung back to the North, passed through West, South West and North again before finally settling on West-South-West as night fell. We had been expecting this after recent weather forecasts and considered anchoring in one of the bays. After some discussion the decision was taken to battle on since the wind did not look like becoming a real Buster, but, as so often happened, the darkness excited the wind and gave us a busy night. At midnight we reefed the main and the mizzen. At 0300 we dropped the staysail as the wind reached Force seven but we flew it again at 0630, this time with two reefs. At 0800 we went onto a starboard tack with our staysail reefs shaken out and at 1300 we were back on a port tack. The slackening South Westerly sent us scurrying to shake out our remaining reefs and at tea time, as we sighted Cape Infanta, we were anxiously trying to use every puff of a Force one to keep a course which would clear Cape Agulhas, the very tip of Africa. If only the wind would free a little and help us round. If it did not oblige, we might spend a long night tacking to go nowhere, our backs to a lee shore. The South Westerly increased a little and I glared at the compass as I pointed as high as I could - 250°. We would have to do better than that.

At 0100 Andy spotted the Agulhas Light and did some frantic calculations. The wind freed a little, enabling me to steer 230°. Two hours later, at the end of my watch, the compass heading was 220° and the wind was from the South so we would be free to bear away round Cape Agulhas after another fifteen miles. Then came a sudden panic. Ahead were two lights which did not appear to be moving. They remained equidistant from each other and we were closing with them rapidly. Andy studied the chart for something we might have missed while I peered through the binoculars. Suddenly it dawned on us that the pattern of lights indicated one fishing boat towing another. We could not afford to risk bearing away inshore towards the rocks so we were forced to turn on the engine and head into the wind to pass in front of the towing boat.

In grey daylight we saw nothing of the low lying rocky outcrop of Agulhas but acknowledged its presence with satisfaction and turned our attention to the more familiar, dramatic silhouette of the Cape of Good Hope which we looked forward to glimpsing before too long. The wind was now from the South East again, thrusting us on with increasing ferocity. As it reached Force eight we were bowling along in an exciting seascape of wave crests that frothed and gurgled across False Bay. Sometimes Christian Bugge's bow would plunge into a trough just as a breaking wave towered over us, but the old timbers seemed to be enjoying themselves, always leaping up again to conquer the angry ocean. Now, as we rose on the crests, we saw the Cape's majestic outline in hazy sunlight. We were moving very fast, averaging seven knots, with triple reefed main and number two jib set inboard in the staysail position. Under a clear sky I enjoyed being on deck and feeling the energy of the elements which clashed and yet harmonised in a thrilling display. The water looked its darkest and deepest below me at the rail but away to the skyline the foaming tops reminded me of an Arctic scene. I experienced a childish delight, reminiscent of my first time on a Big Dipper in Blackpool. I put my trust in the muscles of Andy, John and Martin who steered in turn, wrestling the ship back onto course as the waves threw us sideways. Their eyes followed the compass needle and tell-tales alternately, in an effort to keep Christian Bugge on a broad reach. Those of us who were not concentrating on steering, eyed the stress points in the rigging as the wind increased to Force nine. We were being blown too far off shore and therefore needed to go from the present port gybe to a starboard gybe but in these conditions it was a risky manoeuvre. To come round with the wind on the stern would put a lot of pressure on the rigging and on the crew who would be trying to control the boom as it went from one side to the other. "We'll take her through the wind", yelled Andy above the roaring. "Check for trailing ropes". Obediently we looked over the side and gave the all clear. The engine

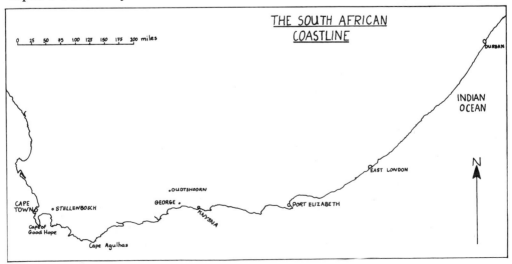

THE SOUTH AFRICAN COASTLINE

0 25 50 75 100 125 150 175 200 miles

DURBAN

INDIAN OCEAN

N

EAST LONDON

·OUDTSHOORN

CAPE TOWN
· STELLENBOSCH

GEORGE ·
KNYSNA

PORT ELIZABETH

Cape of Good Hope

Cape Agulhas

*Rounding the Cape in Force nine
and sunshine.*

*Andy and Iain keep their
safety lines clipped on as
they share the watchkeeping
in blustery weather.*

An aerial view of Table Bay.

*From M-Berth we could
look across from our
steering position to the
larger ocean going yachts.*

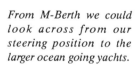

sprang to life and we went to our stations. I took the wheel while Andy and Iain braced themselves to haul in on the main sheet. Martin and John manned the jib sheet and got ready to change the runners. "Start bringing her round", shouted Andy from behind me. I heaved the wheel to port and heard the ratchet of the winch which held a turn of the main sheet. Martin leaned back almost to deck level with the effort of hauling in on the jib sheet while John lugged the heavy blocks of the starboard runner back to the runner chain plate, staggering against the deckhouse as he went. Gradually the boat came up into the wind, our hull wallowing and the sails flogging like mad. The steering position was now a mass of rope with the main sheet from the six part pulley system as tight as it would go. "Tighten that runner", roared Andy to John, then to me, "Take her over gently". I kept going to port and had difficulty staying on my feet as we began to take the force of the wind on our starboard side. Steadily the jib sheet and main sheet were eased until we came round onto the required course. I switched the engine off and sighed with relief. "Isn't it lunchtime?" inquired John.

It was about this time that we started picking up Pan Pan radio calls. All shipping was asked to look out for any survivors of a fishing boat which was thought to have sunk in the gales. We kept a special watch for the rest of the day.

Hout Bay came into view and, with the coming of darkness, pin-points of light around Table Bay. The wind kept up its intensity but now it was accompanied by squalls which sent lashing rain and howling gusts off the mountains. The problem now seemed to be one of finding a way of slowing the ship down and lowering the sails in safety. We headed close into the lee of the land where the ridge known as the 'lion's rump' afforded some protection. Here we tamed the thrashing canvas and sheeted the boom hard down on the gallows. As we entered Cape Town Harbour we began to think we had been dreaming because the dock-lights were mirrored in calm water and the air was still. We tied up alongside Globe Wall at 0015, weary but unable to wind down to the threshold of sleep for some while. I lay awake regretting the fact that my first impression of Cape Town did not include the daylight splendour of Table Mountain.

As the sun filtered through the saloon windows later that morning, I found myself unable to relax sufficiently to lie in. On deck I gazed at the mountain I had longed to see and understood why people find it so impressive. Its stark outline towers above the city, creating an aura of strength and beauty. The chug of a motor made me turn in time to see Roi de Soleil entering the harbour with Lulu, Gigi and Anique looking cold and drawn in sweaters and thick socks. Sandpiper followed, looking equally forlorn but both crews managed a smile as the early morning sun began to thaw their fingers and toes. Their small boats had taken a pounding in the heavy seas and Lulu was most concerned about his damaged radio.

His story slotted in with ours like this....

He had been well ahead of Christian Bugge when the forecast for Westerlies came through. He decided to head for the sheltered anchorage just behind Cape Agulhas, in company with Sandpiper. This would have proved a wise move if it had not been for the fact that the wind turned Southerly as the night wore on. Whilst it helped us on our way, it presented a problem for the two anchored yachts. Both were forced to keep a continuous anchor watch because they were now on a lee shore and they could not risk leaving the bay in the dark because it was littered with the remains of a wrecked tanker. After a traumatic night, they escaped at dawn, rounded Cape Agulhas and spent twenty four hours battling with the strong winds and heavy seas. Now they were somewhat surprised to find us already in port.

The Royal Cape Yacht Club made us very welcome. We were given a free stay because of a reciprocity agreement with the Seychelles Yacht Club and we were allowed to move to M-Berth where the Round-the-World Yachts are often moored. Admittedly, our particular corner seemed to accumulate a great deal of flotsam and jetsam but a company of cormorants thought it a very special spot indeed. Even the occasional seal surfaced in the dark brown water.

On our first evening in port, we monopolised the Royal Cape payphone for an hour while we followed up names that had been given to us by friends and relatives. We opened the conversation tentatively, trying to find a simple way of introducing ourselves and then suggesting that perhaps they would like to come and see the boat. Much to our surprise, these strangers, linked to us only by mutual friends in distant places, sounded enthusiastic about meeting us. They even began to talk of visits to their homes, seemingly undaunted by the knowledge that we numbered eight!

Our diary began to fill up as we arranged for each family to join us on Christian Bugge for tea or coffee and it filled up even more as they offered to take us for a drive or help with the shopping. We ate sumptuous barbecues, watched videos, played with family pets and generally experienced a complete break from the spartan regime of Christian Bugge. By way of a thank you, we always tried to go armed with a small gift such as a chocolate cake or iced flapjacks. Iain's current specialities were South African koeksistas - little twists of deep fried dough dipped in syrup. These were a particular favourite with us and our hosts. In order to make them in sufficient quantities to satisfy our gluttony, Iain usually enlisted the help of Lucy and Joan who enjoyed plaiting the fingers of dough. As the master baker, he would stand by with the hot fat and a super critical eye.

Every day held some excitement. One of our contacts was Gareth de Jong, a harbour pilot who was kind enough to take some of us for a circular drive past Fish Hoek and Hout Bay, returning to Cape Town via a spectacular road cut into the rock face along the coast. We stopped at all the viewing points and encountered the bold baboons of the Cape Peninsula. Gareth also took us to his office high up in the administrative tower which commands a panoramic view of Table Bay. Here we met others of the twenty one harbour pilots and heard tales of wrecks, drownings and general dockside gossip.

On most of our excursions we numbered only seven for Martin was busy renewing old friendships. He had decided to stick with us on the long haul to the Caribbean so I suppose he was making the most of his two weeks in port. He too monopolised the payphone - "Hello Carol?.......(in very jocular tones) This is Martin. Remember - we met a year ago when I was heading East? ....(somewhat deflated) Oh - congratulations. Well, maybe I'll see you around sometime ...... Sure. Bye." Philosophically he replaced the receiver and consulted his list of names. At last he managed to contact a girl he had met in Knysna and whose mother owned a vineyard to the East of Cape Town. This phonecall yielded more success and it soon became apparent that the attractions were not only the grapes! Later, as we prepared to cast off warps on March 12th, their tender and restrained farewell prompted Lucy to record in her diary, 'If there weren't so many people around, I'm sure Martin would have said goodbye properly'.

We could not leave Cape Town without climbing the Mountain. We picked a clear day and trained and bused our way to Kirstenbosch Gardens from where we could follow the recommended route up through Skeleton Gorge. It was a steep but shady scramble to the top of the Gorge, where we were rewarded with a magnificent view from Breakfast Rock. It was another hour or so to Maclear's Beacon, the highest point, at 1088 metres. The whole climb had taken us three hours and it was a further thirty minutes walk to the Cable Station where we ambled around the viewing stages before risking our lives in the Cable Car for the descent.

The other expedition we felt compelled to undertake was a visit to Stellenbosch. For this we hired a big old Ford and headed first to the town of Stellenbosch. Andy drove but had the wind taken out of his sails when he was stopped for speeding on an invitingly long, straight stretch of road. The policeman was quite matter-of-fact about it and told us that the case would not come to court until the middle of April. We breathed again, for we all knew we would be far from land by then. We lingered in the Brandy Museum and then stopped off at Weisenhof Game Reserve to see wildebeests, cape hartebeests, cheetahs, buffaloes, zebras etc. before catching a tour of the Van Ryn Brandy Cellars. Here, in a stately grey building of chateau character, a well informed young lady showed us an instructive film on the distillation of brandy. We trailed behind her as she led us through the cellars and talked of the blending and maturation necessary to create that golden

The Van Ryn building.

elixir - brandy - soul of the grape and heart of the wine. We were mesmerised by her smooth talk and then jolted into laughter as a little old man demonstrated the art of coopering. He tapped the metal bands into place with lively rhythms and twinkling eyes - a real showman. We expected to be shown the way out but no, the tour had not ended. We filed into the plush room where we had started. Rows of glasses and little plates of savoury biscuits awaited us. Bottles appeared. "I think you'll notice the complex nose of this one", said the authoritative voice. Of course we did. We also noticed a complex glowing of the cheeks as we headed out into the brilliant sunlight of the afternoon. We felt guilty that we had not tasted any wine in this famous area, so, before starting for Cape Town, we stopped at one of the vineyards. I believe one Rand entitled us to to a taste of five wines. We paid three Rand and shared the little glasses amongst the eight of us.

Looking back on our two weeks in Cape Town, I still find it incredible that so many people paused in their daily routine to offer hospitality to a motley bunch of complete strangers. On one occasion a man stopped to admire the ship and ended up asking us to his home for a meal the next day! He was just one of a steady stream of interested visitors. When a doctor turned up, I raised the question of whether to carry penicillin injections on long voyages. This had been nagging me ever since my appendicitis and was now worrying me considerably with the prospect of several weeks in mid ocean. He agreed that it was a wise precaution and next day produced the appropriate equipment. I felt better knowing that we had the penicillin for I knew that antibiotics in capsule form did not suit every occasion. However, the thought of actually using the syringes in an emergency, horrified me. Quickly I stowed the box out of sight.

A chill black evening enveloped Table Bay as Gareth waved us away from the quayside in a gusty blow. Beyond the harbour, the wind settled to a steady Force four. Mechanically we raised the sails, our limbs heavy from the indolence of port life and our hearts weighed with goodbyes and thoughts of the long sail ahead. Few words were necessary. Each person knew intuitively what was needed and the only instruction was a slight body movement indicating a wrinkle in the mainsail. Automatically the peak was slackened off a fraction. The course was set for St. Helena and the watchkeepers took charge, leaving the rest of the crew free to get some sleep.

It was a shark which roused us from our first day blues. John's breakfast watch had hardly begun when the commotion in the water astern of us threw the crew into confusion. "We've hooked a shark!" shrieked Martin. The message was relayed from stern to stem and Iain staggered up on deck, trying to shake the sleep off him. Martin and Andy shouted for a variety of implements while the rest of us dithered excitedly, like hens confronted by a fox. Together, Martin and Andy hauled on the line and brought the angry looking mouth of a small shark close to the boat. We estimated that it was only four to six feet long but we lacked the right equipment for catching such beasts. The strain showed on Andy's face as he and Martin made a supreme effort to pull 'Jaws' over the bulwark rail. He, sensing that it was his last chance, writhed in a desperate struggle and was suddenly gone, taking with him Iain's new octopus lure. Two days later, in complete contrast we found a small squid on the line and were so eager for the taste of the sea that we cut the poor little thing into rings and fried him for breakfast.

We had light-to-moderate Southerly winds all the way to St Helena, which meant comfortable sailing and no panics except once when the mainsail suddenly lowered itself, making a disturbing noise at the normally quiet hour of 2300. A bolt which connected the gaff jaws to the throat halyard block, had broken but this was soon rectified and the voyage continued at its gentle pace. The wind and waves were so predictable that the helmsman managed to read a book, steer the ship and keep watch, all at the same time. As we progressed Northwards, the warmer air encouraged us to relax on deck more often, the bustle and sophistication of Cape Town far behind us now.

Dinette and galley showing seating in the foreground, cooker and freezer with lifting fiddled top, behind. The passage to the engine room leads off to the right of the freezer.

An Island on its Own

Two weeks out of Cape Town, on Tuesday March 27th, the severe coastline of St. Helena rose up steeply before us and at 0930 we anchored off Jamestown - a settlement held in the cleft of two barren slopes. The wind funnelled through the opening and buffeted the few vessels that were anchored in the exposed waters.

Our first task was to contact John Rogers whom we had known in the Seychelles and who was now working in St. Helena as one of a British team trying to get the fishing industry underway. The Port Authority relayed a message to him which brought him to the quayside to greet us as we negotiated the difficult dinghy landing. As the swell rose to the level of the steps, passengers had to reach for one of the ropes suspended there for that purpose and quickly step ashore - remembering of course to secure their bags to their arm, for there was often no second chance. Over a glass of beer in a sunny courtyard, we exchanged news and arranged to meet at Ann's Place for a meal on the following evening. It seemed we had only just got there in time for John was due to leave for England on Thursday to collect his wife and three children. He was going on the local supply boat, The R.M.S. St. Helena, to Cape Town and thence by plane.

The meal at Ann's Place which turned out to be an informal restaurant under an awning in a backyard, was good and plentiful with the accent on fish dishes. As we drank local beer and soft drinks, we gathered some information about St. Helena and its population, often known as 'Saints'.

The island was first discovered by a Portuguese, Joao da Nova, but became inhabited when the East India Company ran it and used it as a revictualling station for their ships, hence a very mixed population descended from Africans, Indians, Europeans and others who had come over from the mainland. The age of steam turned it into a coaling station and in 1834 the island was handed over to Britain as a Crown Colony. Right now the whole population was preparing to celebrate this glorious one hundred and fifty years of British Rule with an impending visit from Prince Andrew on April 4th - just a few days after we hoped to be gone. Although the spoken language is english, it has developed from the speech of sailors during the eighteenth and nineteenth centuries and has retained a broad rural sounding lilt which is difficult to understand at full speed. John Rogers told us that newcomers are often shocked by the swear words which are used liberally by everyone as a matter of course. I detected an American twang amongst some of the men who had served on Ascension, approximately seven hundred miles to the North West.

During the next two days we saw as much of the island as possible. Jamestown is little more than a village, with a main street running away from the sea to a small residential area clustered around the road which winds out of the town and on into the hilly interior. The people were easy going and obliging, preoccupied with the forthcoming week of celebrations. Decorations were going up and a wooden platform was being constructed near the Governor's official residence. The time I chose to do the ship's washing at the tap on the steps of the quayside, happened to coincide with the school children's rehearsal for Prince Andrew. I was surrounded by laughing faces as I pummelled two week's dirt away to the words of their special song - "We welcome you, Prince Andrew, to the land we love so well.......". In her enthusiasm the music teacher danced backwards and tripped over my washing! I doubt whether they would let me crouch here amongst the suds on April 4th.

St. Helena welcomed yachties but did expect some remuneration and I suppose you can hardly blame them. An island on its own in the middle of a wide ocean is able to call the tune. That did not stop us being shocked at the sixteen pound harbour dues, especially in view of the fact that there wasn't a harbour! On top of this charge was a landing fee of one pound per person, though some people might have considered that it was they who should be paid for making that daring jump! It was the custom for the police to hold all passports until departure - a good way of ensuring that they got their money. Four days was not long enough to eat our way through enough cheddar cheese to recoup the value of those charges but the price did give us some comfort. It was heavily subsidised at eighty pence

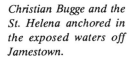

Christian Bugge and the St. Helena anchored in the exposed waters off Jamestown.

per pound - surely a lot cheaper than England even in 1984. We obtained our supply from Mrs Solomon's shop, along with crusty bread. John became really happy as he feasted on his favourite food.

The hens of St. Helena were not so happy. I had assumed that there would be a plentiful supply of eggs in a rural community like that. How stupid I was. We soon heard that every hen on the island was on strike and there was not one egg to be had! On board, our remaining six eggs from a Cape Town supermarket were treated like gold dust. In fact we treasured them so carefully that I was able to use three of them in Lucy's birthday cake a month later!

Pat decided that she and Joan would take a taxi tour of St. Helena in company with other yachties. Andy and I looked at the map and concluded we would get more out of a walking tour, even though we might not cover as much ground. Iain and Lucy were also keen to walk so the four of us set out at 7.00a.m. armed with sustaining sweets and a packed lunch.

We headed out of Jamestown via the Jacob's Ladder, a steep flight of 699 steps up the side of a cliff face which was originally a hauling point for canons used in the defence of the island. As we puffed our way to the top, some of the local lads came towards us at frightening speed as their seats skimmed the hand rails from top to bottom.

We went on climbing to the South, past very poor houses with bleak aspect and little vegetation but as we reached High Knoll Fort at five hundred and eighty four metres, a more fertile landscape unfolded itself through misty drizzle. We dipped down into tranquil woodland, much like Devon countryside and peered through the trees at Plantation House, the Governor's private residence. Now we turned East through pretty valleys and the Devil's Punchbowl where we saw acres of the flax which covers much of the central region of St. Helena, reminiscent of more prosperous times when this was a valuable commodity. Around midday we reached Longwood House where Napoleon was held in exile for six years and where he died in 1821. The French flag fluttered above us, indicating French control of this sacred territory. The old retainer stopped mowing the lawns and came to greet us. Proudly, he opened up the house and showed us what had been his domain for over thirty years. We listened to the touching story of Napoleon's friendship with a lady in a neighbouring house and imagined him riding over the hills in isolated freedom. We were impressed by the sight of the exile's bed and the blood spot on the billiard table where he was laid out in death. We signed the visitor's book while the old man gave us his character reference and told us where and how he was to stand during Prince Andrew's visit. He didn't quite hold out his hand but since admission to the house was free, we did not begrudge him a token of our appreciation. Pat, Joan and the others arrived just as we completed our tour and we all lunched in sunshine on the lawn.

After the break, we retraced our steps past the small settlement of Longwood, where there seemed to be more donkeys than people and turned North towards Napoleon's Tomb. Looking back, I am not quite sure why we visited a clearing in the middle of nowhere, with a square of black railings enclosing nothing but wild flowers. Perhaps it was because all visitors were expected to make this

Longwood House is maintained by France in memory of Napoleon's exile there.

pilgrimage. I suppose the place had a dank atmosphere of its own - the suggestion of the ghost of a small man who made a big impact on the world. I forget how long the body remained there before the French collected it.

We had now walked about nine miles and were following long hairpins down the main route into Jamestown. Gladly we accepted a lift for the last mile or two and the driver of the small car took the opportunity to tell us about her visits to England. Why is it that the people of St. Helena feel such a strong allegiance to a country which does very little for them? There is some farming of crops and animals on a small scale but this does not offer much scope for young people. Updating of schools is a slow business. Entertainment is limited. The cinema is a shack with wooden seats and ancient photographs on the walls. Otherwise, amusement has to be simple and homespun. Some enterprising young people extricate themselves from the island in search of higher qualifications but because their passports are not British they do not automatically have the right to reside in their mother country. They feel British, their currency is Sterling and yet they are denied British nationality! For politicians to be worried about the influx of a few 'Saints' seems to me to be the height of pomposity or racial prejudice. It's not as if the whole population would suddenly want to move to England for most are content with their peaceful way of life without television, aeroplanes and high technology but they would surely welcome recognition as British subjects.

It's to be hoped that the fishing projects are providing a boost to their economy for St. Helena is surrounded by a treasure trove of tuna, particularly Albacore, the king of tuna fish. We were fascinated to watch the local men catching these big ones with just a pole tipped with an unbarbed hook. They simply agitated the surface of the water with the pole to attract the tuna and then flipped them up into the boat as their mouths closed on the hook. It looked easy the way they did it - and so fast. Sometimes they dropped one in the boat and arched the pole back into the water to catch another without a break. John Rogers was involved with experiments in drying and salting and as we walked along the quayside, he pointed to boxes of fish which had been declared unsatisfactory.

It was pleasantly warm in St. Helena and we began to think of discarding our snug sleeping bags once again for we only ever used sheet bags in the Tropics. Foolishly, I hung some of them on deck and came up to find that Iain's sleeping bag had disappeared altogether - claimed by one of those gusts which whistled through the valleys. I had not intended to discard it quite so completely. Luckily, Iain never seemed to feel the cold. Even in the worst weather he rarely wore a sweater and his size ten feet with their splayed toes were never pushed into boots.

Topping up with water was a 'carry the can' job because big boats cannot go close into the quay. We borrowed extra containers and made numerous trips to ensure that we left with full tanks. Boats had been known to wallow in the Doldrums for weeks without rain so conservation of water was now a priority as we upped anchor and waved goodbye to land for thirty three days. The fortress-like outline of St. Helena with steep cliffs on all sides and an area of only 47 square miles, receded into the distance. Once more we were on our own.

"Can you tell me the way to Napoleon's Tomb?"

The Christian Bugge Academy.

On April 3rd, three days out of St. Helena, I felt moved to remember Christian Bugge's famous rescue which took place forty six years previously. I composed a song with what I thought was a stirring tune. Lucy, Joan and I had a captive audience at tea time for its first performance...........

Heaving, rolling through the swell,
Cutting the water you know so well,
Topsail up and pulling proud,
Headsails strain to touch the cloud.
Fly, fly with heavy grace,
Gentle old lady live again.
Dream, dream of long ago,
Battling with the sea for ships and men.

April 3rd in thirty eight,
Rokta's men await their fate.
Waves like mountains batter the ship,
Hold her in their fearful grip.
Die, die perhaps we'll die
Dragged beneath the angry foam.
Dream, dream of loving hands
Reaching out to take us home.

Christian Bugge hears the call,
Storming out to save them all,
Captain Bakken steady and brave
Stop at nothing men to save.
Fly, fly to Rokta's aid,
Heed not the storm which threatens you.
Dream, dream of fireside warmth
Holding someone close to you.

Rokta now a broken ship,
Half is left and soon to slip,
Crew is desperate, glimpsing death,
Fighting spray to take a breath.
Cry, cry for wasted youth,
News is transmitted throughout the land.
Dream, dream that your loved one
Will return to touch your hand.

How can any ship get near,
Every man trembling with fear,
Bakken says it's time to go,
Speed and courage we must show.
Try, try the shallows to cross,
Choose the biggest waves to ride.
Hurl, hurl the rescue lines,
Dare not go too near her side.

Men are jumping off the wreck,
Greedy ocean swallows the speck,
Rokta glides to Neptune's Land,
Rescue crew reach out their hand.
Cry, cry for wasted youth,
Six are saved and six are dead.
Dream, dream of tranquil seas,
Never a storm for man to dread.

Often, our regular music lessons were held on deck in good weather. I used to sit on the side deck with my back against the chartroom and a pile of books on my lap, while Lucy and Joan sprawled either side of me. We took it in turns to choose a song, switching from 'The wraggle taggle gypsies' to 'Dis long time gal me never see yu', to 'What shall we do with the drunken sailor', with hardly a pause for breath. Sometimes we tried three part rounds or solo verses just to vary the programme. Occasionally, Lucy or Joan, or even both of them would have the sulks because they thought I had been unfair or because they did not like the chosen song. In that case, I found myself singing solo until the mood changed, which it always did.

Sulks were not uncommon. After all, the confined space of a boat at sea is bound to create some kind of tension. Joan got rid of her tension with the occasional tantrum. Sometimes in the schoolroom she had miserable battles with her mother over maths and English, which had the effect of making Lucy smug about her completed exercises. Predictably, this riled Joan even more and an argument ensued over the allocation of table space, each one glowering like a cornered bull. Joan's worst tantrums occurred in port, possibly because she had come to expect such a lot from each landfall that it was rather a disappointment to find that the

This stamp was issued to mark CB's notable service in the Norwegian Rescue Service.

«Christian Bugge» var en utrolig god båt i dårlig vær.

Clip from a Norwegian newspaper in 1938 showing Christian Bugge heading out into the storm to save the crew of Rokta.

adults were unable to go sightseeing every minute of the day. When Joan was really in the mood to seek attention, she would turn on the taps, wind herself up and make everyone's life a misery with shouts and screams. Lucy's rebelliousness was usually much quieter but there were moments when her exasperation with Joan or Iain exploded with a fury that was none too silent.

Down below in the dinette, the senior schoolroom never erupted like this but if I happened to be baking bread in the galley, Iain could not stop himself wittering on and on about any topic that entered his head. Suddenly I would realise that half the morning had gone by and that he could hardly have achieved any school work, so I willed myself not to answer him or look at him unless he required help with a subject. The grades and comments he obtained from the tutors of Mercer's College who supplied his correspondence course, were excellent, proving that he must have got the work done sometime. Inevitably one big drawback was the time lapse between posting the completed work and receiving the corrected papers. For instance, the package sent in February from Cape Town had to be returned to Trinidad, our next poste restante address, almost three months later. Always we had to try and envisage where we would be at a certain time and write accordingly to all concerned. Apart from the social aspect of being without company of his own age, Iain was missing out on computers and practical sciences. We knew it might be a struggle when we arrived back in England but at least I was sure he was keeping up with his age group in maths, English, French and geography. I couldn't help worrying about whether we had done the right thing in keeping him out of the school system for so long. Was he really approaching fifteen this year? Would he adapt to the classroom again? Would he make friends easily? Would Andy ever be able to get a job in Britain again? If so, where? Would Iain appreciate the voyage in retrospect or would he resent it? These queries nagged my brain from time to time but then I would put the other point of view to myself. Surely he was gaining so much from the trip itself - navigation, self reliance, a glimpse of other countries and cultures. Still, I couldn't be sure. Lucy didn't worry me for she was three years younger and would be just coming up to secondary age at the end of the trip. Wherever she started school she would be with other new children. Besides, she was extremely adaptable and was obviously enjoying the travelling. Iain was a darker horse.

Afternoon craft sessions in the junior schoolroom were a joy to everyone until it came to the clearing up. In the hush of siesta time for those who needed extra sleep, Joan, Lucy and occasionally Iain created miscellaneous pictures and nick-nacks from odds and ends. The saloon table became littered with newspaper, pipe cleaners, scraps of material, glue and scissors, as the spirit of creativity took over. During our ten month voyage, these sessions produced night-dress cases, peg dolls, beaded food covers, decorated eggs, dolly book ends weighted with sand from the Azores, prints from lino cuts, stuffed animals from special sewing kits, book markers and various Christmas cards and decorations. One day we really went to town with a Bugge badge. The land masses were cut from scraps of coloured felt and the route was marked with running stitches. While I was helping the children I made one for myself which now has pride of place in my jewellery drawer. In Port Elizabeth Iain did a special Christian Bugge lino cut from which we printed nearly one hundred Christmas cards to send to our friends all over the world.

Neither Lucy nor Joan found drawing easy. Both seemed to have reached a stage where they needed a great deal of reassurance to even try. They had lost the spontaneity of earlier years when they drew freely, without anxiety over the result. Joan would talk and talk about what she was going to do and how she was going to do it, then, as she drew her first lines she would lose all her confidence and go mad with the rubber. Lucy would often start better but become inhibited if she thought anyone was laughing at her picture. They each did a distinctive charcoal drawing of a cat which looked down at us from the display area in the saloon for many weeks. In Port Elizabeth they drew the shape of a church which could be seen from the deck of Christian Bugge as she sat high on the slipway. Mostly they enjoyed making collage pictures or painted patterns. The acrylic paints in tubes proved easy to use, mixed well and produced clear bright colours for a variety of work. Since their mixing palettes were usually dinner plates, there was always a rush to scrub them clean before the evening meal.

French lessons were fun because we would talk, play games and sing catchy phrases to make the words stick. I did no written work with Joan and only a little with Lucy. Each of the girls had separate taped lessons for which I would borrow Iain's small personal cassette player so that we could listen with headphones. These funny little stories made the world of difference to their French and indeed mine as well! Once, for tea time entertainment, we put on a French play using vocabulary that was familiar to both girls. I think we just about got to the end before collapsing in hysterics as, 'pauvre petit Minet' was found 'sous la casserole'.

In the morning study periods Pat gave them a thorough grounding in maths and English, with individual attention that can never be achieved in a normal school. She inspired them with imaginative ideas for compositions which were sometimes read out as a tea time treat. Geography accompanied us in a natural way. Everyone joined in the teaching of this subject as we discussed planets and stars, formation and vegetation of the different islands, weather patterns, volcanoes and earthquakes etc. These were lessons they experienced and absorbed in a way they could never do in a classroom, however good the teacher or the visual aids. Iain benefited from this broad spectrum but at the same time studied less relevant topics in more depth as his lesson notes demanded.

The thirty three days between St. Helena and Trinidad constituted the most sustained learning period of the 'Christian Bugge Academy for Young Ladies and Gentleman'. Weekends were not observed, according to our system of 'school at sea, holiday in port'. The only relaxation of the rule was for Lucy's birthday when the youngest were allowed to boss the wisest. We played games for most of the day. John seemed quite glad to escape on deck when it was his turn to go on watch but he was not to be let off that easily. He was expected to sing loudly for 'pass the parcel' and stop periodically for the lucky person with the parcel to discard a wrapper, claim a sweet, and read his forfeit. Refusal to run round the deck, stand on one's head, or sing Old King Cole to the tune of Waltzing Matilda meant forfeiting one's sweet! Nobody refused. Andy won the star prize at the centre of the package — a small tin of grapefruit juice. Lucy noted all the edible treats of the day in her diary - popcorn and three layer birthday cake for tea, ice cream (made from a packet mix) and chocolate sauce for pud. She went to bed, surrounded by home made cards and presents. The bracelet which Martin had fashioned from thin cord now adorned the wrist which drew me down for a good-night kiss. The dress which I had managed to stitch in secret moments with matching bag, purse and hairband, had been hung up with unusual care, and Joan's present, a necklace made of boiled and coloured fish vertebrae adorned the light bracket over the bunk. Her eyes told me she had had a happy day.

The very next morning dawned with a hiccup. In her diary, Lucy recorded with indignation......... 'The steering broke and the men woke Joan and I with the noise they made mending it. As the men had messed up the saloon mending the steering, we had to work in the dinette'. From my point of view it was not quite so simple. At 0500 I was steering a steady course when suddenly a sharp twang came from somewhere beneath my feet and the steering wheel revolved ineffectually in my hand. I yelled for help and we immediately hove to under staysail and mizzen while Andy crawled into the stern cavity to begin the task of connecting a replacement steering cable on the port side. It took four and a half hours of sweated labour and complete disruption of the saloon while the bulkhead panels were removed to expose the link-up to the steering wheel. To the girls this was simply an inconvenience which they tolerated grudgingly, and on reflection I think this was probably the best attitude. If they had been as involved as I was, they would have had panicky thoughts like mine......supposing Andy can't mend it (Andy usually could mend things)......or a gale blows up (the wind was a steady Force three)......supposing we hit a ship (our radio was working perfectly and there was nothing on the horizon)......or it breaks again in more difficult circumstances

Lucy and Joan share craft materials in the saloon during afternoon school.

(highly unlikely, but also possible as we discovered six weeks later in Jamaica). Repairs completed, we sped on towards Trinidad.

From time to time on the voyage, I took my own education in hand and made a point of taking sun-sights in order to correct our position, found by dead reckoning. At first I became infuriated because I could not master the knack of keeping the sun in the telescope. Either I swore at the boat for moving just when I had brought the sun down to touch the horizon, or I became completely confused because the sun had mysteriously disappeared. My squinting eyes left the sextant, only to see a bank of cloud obliterating the target. The calculations gave me another problem, for I had a mental block about using those boring tables until slowly, I began to understand the reasons for the various corrections. (Andy always told me that teachers make the worst pupils.) It was an exciting moment when I could do all the working out for myself, put a dot on the chart and say, "That's where I think we are". I compared notes with Iain who was also learning to navigate, and with practice, we both learnt to use the sextant with competence in fair conditions. The girls grew accustomed to looking at the lumps and bumps marked on the charts and they liked to check the days run - anything from twenty five miles in the Doldrums to a fast run of 164 in livelier waters. Lucy also learnt to use the dividers to estimate how far it was to our next landfall.

Even on our longest hauls we did not worry too much about physical exercises. Crossing oceans in Christian Bugge could not be compared with sailing the suicidal bath tubs which we sometimes saw in port. After all, we had a large open deck, stairs from deck level to chartroom and from saloon to dinette, full standing headroom down below and separate cabins, so the ordinary activities of the day provided sufficient exercise to keep our bodies in good working order. However, now and then we had a fitness fling, often because the girls asked for a P.E. lesson. We would run up and down on the spot, do star jumps, press ups, and even high kicks! I say 'we' but I don't ever remember Andy or John joining us in such strenuous activities. They preferred to conserve their energy for when it was really needed, so they said. None of us had much flab to fight. We were all well toned up by constant tensing of the muscles as we braced ourselves against the movement of

Andy and John mend the sails on our 33 day passage to Trinidad.

Iain added interesting detail to his certificate for Lucy.

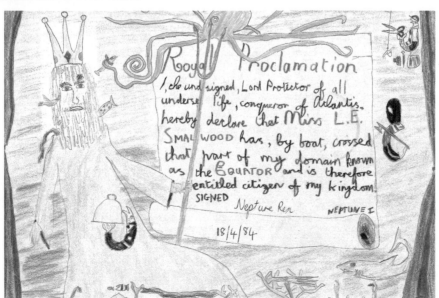

the ship. Our rounded relatives who met us in Plymouth were somewhat shocked by our lean appearance, although they waited until we had put on weight before telling us how gaunt we had looked on arrival. That's as maybe, but I certainly felt healthier at sea than on land with all its culinary temptations. Iain would claim that he never had enough to eat during our year of travel. He would probably claim that now with two cooked meals a day!

When the sea became glassy and the deck blistered our feet, the girls begged to be allowed to swim. With a long rope tied securely to their waist, they leapt recklessly from the stern into the shimmering blue of three mile deep water, while at least two adults would scan the smoothness for the suspicion of a fin. Iain usually swam as well, teasing the girls into shrieks and giggles. They practised swimming faster than Christian Bugge (not difficult in these conditions) and jumping further than each other until either the wind increased or someone called "Time". I went in once and appreciated a few minutes of cool pleasure on an otherwise tedious and sultry day. We had encountered the Doldrums much sooner than expected - only eleven days out of St. Helena and approximately five degrees South. We made slow progress under a sky which seemed to be pressing down on us. Squalls and fickle winds pushed the boat round in circles. It was as though we were in a giant mixing bowl of the world's weather. After a further nine day struggle to go forwards and not backwards, we judged we were sitting on the equator - wind strength zero. Limp sails slatted with the roll of the boat and I had visions of crisscrossing the equator for days. We cheered ourselves up with festivities. Lucy and Joan had been busy with certificates for Mums and Dads, and Iain was persuaded to join in the activities. In the sweltering heat I secreted Andy into a cabin to dress him in strips of seaweed made from torn newspaper. With a yellow oily hat to set off his thick dark beard, he crept to the forepeak to make his surprise appearance on deck. Joan and Lucy adored the drama. They retreated with great delight as this stern and grizzly Neptune advanced, brandishing a boat hook. "I have come to inoculate you against Deep Sea Fever", he roared. This task completed midst squeals and giggles, he produced a certificate for each crew member to prove they had crossed that special part of his domain. Now the proceedings became rowdy as the girls sneaked up on Neptune with a bucket of water. He was too well prepared. He snatched the bucket before it was raised and dowsed the two of them, which was what they really wanted anyway.

As the sun departed a ruby sky, John fetched the bottle of port we had been saving for this occasion. We needed that tot of optimism after the discovery about the stores......."Here's to a speedy end to the Doldrums and plenty of fish!"

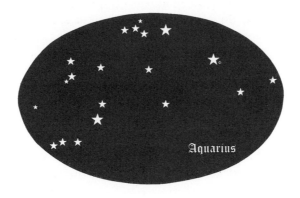

Aquarius

What Happened to the Rice?

In utter disbelief, I tilted the tin and stared at the few grains which shuffled to the corner. This was April 8th, only nine days out of St. Helena, with Trinidad hardly a dream as yet. To discover emptiness where there should have been fifteen kilos of rice denoted a major catering crisis and would certainly bring Pat and I under heavy fire from the rest of the crew. Frantically, I checked the other tins - only flour as I expected. I measured the amount of rice left in our smaller galley store and found only eight cups. To think we had imagined that our initial supply of fifty kilos would last us all the way to England!

Pat was as perplexed as I was. She had not realised that we had been dipping into our last tin. With a tacit understanding that recriminations were pointless at this stage, we laid the facts before the others and suffered Martin's contemptuous looks. "Does it mean turning back to St. Helena?" queried Andy glumly. I went back to the stores book to ponder the problem carefully. Meticulously, I checked each item in the book against the tins and packets actually in the lockers until I had a clear picture of everything that could be eaten. So far rice had been our principle staple food. We had left Cape Town with a sack of potatoes but that was now finished. We had to find an alternative which would provide the bulk in our diet. Our stock of flour was just about adequate for bread, cakes, puddings and pastry so I did not think I could gain much from that line. My finger moved on down the page and stopped at 'oats' - yes of course - that was the answer. A combination of oats and flour might just save the day. For some peculiar reason, we had overstocked the ship with oats, so much so that I had begun to think we had mistaken kilos for pounds. We had about twice as much as we needed for porridge breakfasts. I did some hasty calculations. I could substitute oats for some of the flour in bread, likewise cakes and puddings. Perhaps I could even put oats in pastry and batters. If we were to cut down on rice and cook two cups instead of three, that would give us four meals. There was enough instant mashed potato for four meals and enough spaghetti for five meals, making a total of thirteen altogether. If we improvised with oats, flour and a few packets of chinese noodles which still remained in the galley cupboard, we could probably last out another two weeks or so. We had a small quantity of lentils, split peas and red beans which would help. My eyes were drawn to the net bags hanging above the dinette table - plenty of onions and one or two butternuts left from South Africa.

I announced that it would not be necessary to turn back but that strict rationing would have to be imposed. The groan that answered me made it quite clear that the crew considered themselves to be on starvation rations already. Still, they were glad to be able to keep going and the tension was relieved by an item of news on the radio that the Governor of St. Helena had fallen in the water as he moved forward to greet Prince Andrew! Knowing the quay as we did and imagining the splendid welcome prepared by the school children, the vision of the Governor in full ceremonial regalia losing his balance was so comical that we laughed till we cried. We could not help wondering if the children had managed to keep a straight face, also Prince Andrew. Much as I laughed, I felt sorry for the Governor whose embarrassment was likely to dog him for some time to come.

In went the oats. It became something of a joke to be the first to spot their appearance in the meal. Our pastry mix changed to fifty per cent brown flour and fifty per cent oats. Our fruit crumbles would have delighted a Scotsman and bread became slightly heavier but more interesting with approximately thirty per cent oats.

My standard recipe for sea water bread was as follows:

1. Mix 2 teaspoons sugar and 4 teaspoons dried yeast with 1 cup fresh water (baby bath temperature). Leave to froth for 10 minutes.

2. Place 12 cups flour in a large bowl.

3. Add yeast mixture, 1 1/3 cups fresh warm water, 1 1/3 cups sea water and 1 tablespoon cooking oil to flour.

4. Mix well and knead until smooth (minimum kneading of whole-meal dough produced a coarse cake-like texture which stayed moist and pleased the crew whereas the white flour dough benefited from thorough, vigorous kneading).

5. Cover the bowl and put in a warm place to rise (I found this took anything from 45 minutes to 2 hours, depending on brand of yeast, humidity etc.).

6. When it has doubled in size, punch it down and knead again if necessary. Shape into loaves and leave to rise again for 20 - 30 minutes.

7. Bake in a hot oven until bread is brown on top and sounds hollow when rapped with a knuckle. (I sometimes had difficulty browning the tops in our paraffin oven because the source of heat was at the bottom. I overcame this to a certain extent by removing the loaves from the tins when they were cooked and replacing them upside-down on a shelf for a further 5 minutes. They certainly looked more appetising with a brown crust.)

Every three to four days I made two batches of dough which was enough for eight small loaves. I began the routine immediately after breakfast at 0800. I made a second mix at 0900 so as to stagger the baking times. Lunch time rolls were often a bonus of bread days and I usually set aside a small quantity of dough for a teatime treat. I rolled this into an oblong, dotted it with a little margarine, dried fruit, sugar and cinnamon, then rolled it all up and cut it into eight catherine wheel portions which I left to rise. I varied the finished buns by glazing or icing them according to my mood. Although I always began with the same basic recipe, I sometimes used margarine in place of vegetable oil, or added sugar to the wholemeal bread. Poppy seeds gave extra flavour and texture to crusty rolls, and an otherwise dull meal could be brightened by a plaited loaf. Bread on Bugge came in all shapes, sizes and colours. By making a long thin loaf I could sometimes offer four slices apiece instead of the standard issue of three and although they were not really getting any more to eat, the gullible crew felt pleased with themselves as they reached for the peanut butter or jam. Lucy and Joan, being the youngest, smallest and least active in boat management, were only allowed two slices of bread as a rule. Lucy was usually happy with this but Joan could always eat more. Her dark eyes pleaded with her mother who sometimes passed her an extra morsel.

We had 'light' lunches. To go with our bread there was a thin sliver of cheese, a small piece of corned beef (12oz. can cut into eight), a bowl of soup or a sardine. If by any remote chance someone refused their full ration of bread, several pairs of beady eyes remained watchful until the fate of the last slice had been decided. Iain was known to negotiate private deals - on one occasion a slice of bread for Martin's grapefruit juice - for although he ate well, he did not enjoy bread on its own and regarded grapefruit juice as a special treat since we mostly drank water.

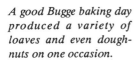

A good Bugge baking day produced a variety of loaves and even doughnuts on one occasion.

If baking day happened to coincide with my early morning watch, and Andy felt able to cope without me for most of the three hours, then I would sometimes begin the bread at 0300. I enjoyed being on my own in a hushed and dimly lit galley, bracing my hip against the motion of the ship as I used both hands to pound the dough. I could spare a few moments in between stages to take the wheel and guard the dawn while Andy checked the charts or read the log. It was easy to bring the crew to breakfast on those mornings Their noses led them to the table.

The salt pork and beef from Durban also had a distinctive smell which emanated from the mast cupboard after one of us had been fishing in the tub. We hacked off about half a pound which was our meat ration for a meal to go round the eight of us, cut it into small strips and soaked it in several changes of sea water. Finally we put it in a little fresh water and then clothed it in lentil or bean sauces to bulk it out. It was good meat, well preserved, but we had lost all our enthusiasm for it by the time we ate the last piece in Fort Lauderdale in July! One alternative to the salt meat was the tinned minced beef in gravy which we had bought in Durban. We stretched one medium tin (14 ounces) by adding onions, split peas and aubergines when we were lucky enough to get them. We had been used to this mushy mixture, perhaps pepped up with curry powder or tomato paste, served on a good dollop of rice. Now, on the St. Helena - Trinidad run, pies and dumplings came into their own. Every few days we would have a real economy meal - oaty dumplings floating in a bowl of soup, followed by oaty peach crumble or sponge pudding made with vinegar and bicarbonate of soda instead of eggs. A friend in Seychelles had put me onto this combination for coating batters and Pat's famous Krazy Kake recipe also used vinegar and bicarb so from these two starting points we concocted volcanic mounds and muddy craters. Failures were gobbled up as fast as successes and woe betide anyone who complained about the size of their portion!

Only Andy could serve out the evening meal. He alone was allowed to cut the pie, spoon out the spuds, slop the gravy, ladle the soup. It had become Bugge law. His judgement was accepted by all, even if there were a few surreptitious looks at the next plate.

White cabbages were a boon. They kept very well, provided they were dry when they were purchased. Usually, we served the chopped raw cabbage with a little onion in french dressing, its crispness complementing the Bugge stews. Our other source of fresh greenery was a supply of mung beans which we sprouted in a plastic container and served in salad or fried rice. Their nutty flavour was equally good on its own or mixed in with a tin of green beans and did a lot to revitalise our taste buds. Unfortunately, I did not always get the growing conditions right and some crops were a failure because they became too wet or too dry but when they were good they were very good.

Pumpkin, butternuts and gemsquash were versatile vegetables with good keeping qualities. Pumpkin soup was an old favourite but the flesh also made a tasty side dish with margarine, onion and seasoning. Butternuts were smaller and pear shaped - best boiled whole. Gemsquash were smaller still, round and greenish, the flesh similar to marrow. Later, when we arrived in Florida, I looked for a similar selection of vegetables but was utterly disappointed both with the selection and the prices. Perhaps we shopped in the wrong places. Our biggest bargains from the United States were special price water melon and yesterday's doughnuts!

The only fruits we ever tried to store for any length of time were apples, oranges, limes, paw-paws (papayas), bananas and grape-fruits. Most of these were made to swing from the chartroom beams in net bags. Here the air could circulate freely around the fruit. When we bought a whole bunch of bananas in Mayotte it swung from the gallows in the shade of the sails and the awning above the steering position.

Our paraffin cooker gave us moments of exasperation, usually when the sea was rough or when Pat or I had planned to make something really special. The familiar fumes penetrated the saloon, followed by muttered curses. The oven burner had extinguished itself at a crucial moment or the kettle and deckhead were being blackened by repeated flare-ups. There was usually a simple solution but not always a speedy one. We got used to the sight of Andy, grimy from paraffin soot, crouched over bits of burner and oven fittings in the middle of the galley, while half cooked food stayed wedged on work tops. To be fair, it did not happen very often. Our stainless steel cooker served us well for eighteen months continual use and it still looks as good as new.

April 21st was a great day for the stores for we caught our first dorade or dolphin fish. This beautiful fish with its domed head and slender body flashed with green, blue and yellow, gave up its life blood on the stern of Christian Bugge and we butchered it for the freezer. The flesh was good but not as full flavoured as tuna or wahoo, our favourites. The catch coincided with a steadying of the wind which we hoped marked the end of the Doldrums at two degrees North. By April 23rd we were running up a daily mileage of between one hundred and fifty and one hundred and sixty five miles. Surely this was tradewind sailing at last. Next day we hooked a large dorade about four feet long and then a small fellow. We were on top of the world. The ocean was suddenly full of activity and the air charged with anticipation. We ran through bizarre belts of choppy water bordered by an oily sea. Martin noticed dust on the rigging and suspected that it came from the Sahara.

On, on we rushed, the North wind becoming more Easterly. We caught a medium sized wahoo and rejoiced at our increasing good fortune. On the last day of April we altered our watches to GMT plus four hours and logged one hundred and sixty two miles.

As we neared civilisation again after over thirty days at sea, the wind lessened and we could only potter towards Port of Spain, identifying the loom of the oil rigs to port and Tobago's Scarborough Light ahead. Then, just to keep us on our toes, a sudden squall sent us screaming through the night of May 3rd. Daylight brought a gentle East wind to coax us past Galera Point along the North coast of Trinidad. We altered course for the high sided narrow channel of the Boca de Monos and noted rapid changes in the colour of the sea. Under engine, we passed through Chaguaramas Bay between Diego Island and Pointe Gourde, inside Five Islands. We tied up at Immigration as dusk became night and prepared for the

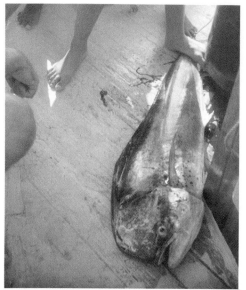

We were fascinated by the beautiful dorade or dolphin fish. Lucy and Joan always watched the butchering of our fish with great interest.

usual formalities. The wide smile of the Trinidadian with silvering frizzy hair was quite compelling - a very different style of Immigration Officer from those in South Africa! Still, even he couldn't help us find much to commend a capital city gilded by oil and a harbour littered with dying ships, whose owners could not quite grasp a share in Trinidad's wealth.

Rich as it is, Port of Spain has awful bread - best quality cotton wool - but I was determined to have a holiday from baking. Our Trinidad dollars could buy little meat for we still adhered to our very tight budget which allowed us to spend no more than the equivalent of seventy five pence on the protein part of the evening meal. Meat was very expensive. Rice, sugar, flour, coffee etc. we bought at a wholesaler's but fresh fruit and vegetables were exorbitant and in short supply. We hoped that our next port of call, Grenada, might have some local produce.

My sightseeing of Trinidad was restricted to a three mile walk to the Hilton Hotel to see a steel band. Faced with an admission charge of ten dollars, Martin, Andy, Iain and I declined courteously. We sneaked up some back stairs to a little balcony overlooking the pool where we gained a free show. The band was impressive but too wholesome. I was looking for that earthy spontaneity of style which I should have realised was not to be found in a tourist hotel. Andy fell asleep.

All in all it seemed sensible to move on quickly, just as soon as Pat, John and Joan had made their excursion to the renowned pitch lake. They returned with chunks of the sticky black stuff which found their way to the girls' clothes lockers and the school cupboard.

Preparations to leave Port of Spain's dock got underway. The Smallwood section of the crew had heavy hearts. News of the death of Andy's father, brought by the British Consul, left us numb. Although Andy spoke to his mother on the telephone, he was deeply sorry not to be with her. Iain and Lucy mourned their grandfather with quiet tears. Trinidad held no happy memories for us.

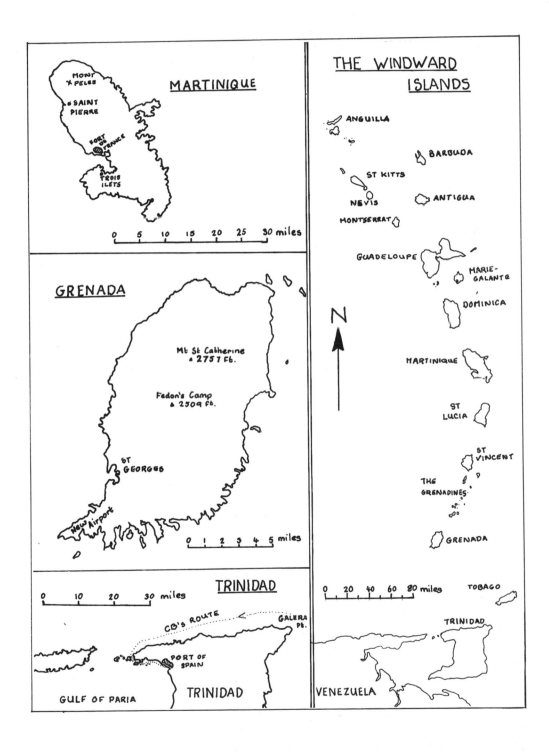

Savouring the East Caribbean

It seemed strange to be leaving green buoys to port. Having had it drummed into me that red buoys are left to port on entering harbour, I was completely thrown by the realisation that Americans do it the opposite way round!

We waved to the U.S. coastguard, hoisted the Red Ensign and headed into the port of St. George on the island of Grenada, less than a day's hop from Port of Spain.

We were interested to take a look at this island which had become the centre of world attention six months previously when the U.S. Marines began the liberation of the Grenadan people from the threat of Red dominance. The murder of political leader, Maurice Bishop, had brought things to a head and after a brief war, the Americans emerged with a halo so big that it must have been difficult to carry!

The way into St. George was narrow. It turned sharply to the right before opening out into a natural harbour where surprisingly big ships were tied up in deep water and where local shallow draught boats adorned a cobbled quay. Later, when exploring on foot, we watched fishermen hauling these boats over at right angles for careening. We were directed to a newly dredged channel which gave access to a separate pool where there was a sprinkling of yachts at anchor and a sparsely attended marina, still under construction. Needless to say, we avoided the marina and dropped our hook in leisurely fashion. Within minutes we were boarded by two smiling lads who offered to take care of us during our stay in Grenada. They were willing to fetch supplies and show us round the town. Gently, we told them we were British - always a good excuse for being poor. Dejectedly, they climbed down into their dinghy and left us to do our own shopping. I suppose it must be difficult to understand the financial problems of a group of people travelling the world in such style! When we stepped ashore, two more persuasive young men held out exquisite jewellery made from black coral. I was sad that we could only admire their work because although their manners were impeccable, their eyes pleaded with us. We found out later that many of those trying to scratch a living from yachties, were former members of the local army, now disbanded in favour of a peace-keeping force drawn from Jamaica and other parts of the Caribbean.

As usual, Christian Bugge's timing was unrivalled. A telephone call revealed that a good friend of John Hook, now working in Grenada, had left the island by plane for leave in U.K. at the precise moment that we had entered the harbour. His Guyanese wife Julia, who had never met John, nobly tackled the situation and arranged a meeting. She took us all under her wing, lent John her car, gave us a wonderful meal and the chance to watch some video films, although the usual peak time power cuts delayed this entertainment until after midnight when our eyes were beginning to close. Julia had three children by her previous marriage, their ages compatible with the junior members of our crew. To them our way of life was a novelty. They raced about the deck and dive bombed each other in the water for possession of the windsurfer board. Julia was small and attractive - coffee skin and dimpling smile. She looked at my greying temples which were a source of annoyance to me and said she envied me my silver flashes!

My impressions of Grenada were of trees heavy with cocoa pods and dripping with nutmegs - a clean town with shabby public buildings, high prices and poverty - friendly people with only a trace of a shadow on their faces. On our drive across the island we had difficulty finding our way because there were no sign posts. The villages remained anonymous, labelled only by slogan covered walls -

In Grenada, Julia took us under her wing.

The Americans made a big impact on the island.

THANK GOD FOR U.S. AND CARIBBEAN HEROES OF FREEDOM. Burnt out lorries decked the verges. Hotels stood empty and faceless, vacated by both tourists and troops. The island seemed to be ticking over, waiting for direction and election. Meanwhile, students of the American School of Medicine jogged along the deserted beaches, whilst the new airport, once started by Cubans, now became a U.S. project. An international airport was an essential part of Grenada's plan for tourism.

The musical treasure I had hoped to find in Trinidad, I discovered by accident in Grenada when the unmistakable pulsing of steel pans peppered the air on a quiet afternoon. I called the girls and we rowed towards the source, an unimposing shed on the other side of the harbour. We hovered on the shore as the rhythms burst out at us, then we plucked up courage to go inside. The players were practising but did not seem to mind us watching. The leader spoke little. With just a word or sometimes a nod from him, the group launched into a theme and developed it while the leader walked round listening to individual pans, sometimes demonstrating a correction or suggestion. As the enthusiasm grew, so did the noise until I expected to see the corrugated roof lift. The music seemed to be a series of improvisations with each pan man working to some inner inspiration of his own which complemented the other parts quite naturally. The silence which followed each piece came as a shock because it was so sudden. Everyone knew instinctively where the end was, although to me the music had not reached a logical conclusion and I had not observed any signal from the leader.

Lucy and Joan grew bolder and wandered from pan to pan studying technique. They were even allowed a go, much to their delight. I suspect that many British school children would prefer to join a steel band rather than a recorder group, given the chance. Children like to use their bodies to make music. Playing steel pans requires that physical involvement. The Grenadan men were stripped to the waist, glistening with sweat as they bent over the shiny cylinders, some shallow and supported on frames, others deeper and free standing. The metallic sounds rippled and bubbled from supple wrists. Heads, shoulders and feet were never still. I felt my own feet and hips moving involuntarily to the infectious rhythms. When the band took a break we slipped out and left them in peace.

*   *   *   *   *

Porpoises escorted Christian Bugge from Grenada and a fresh Easterly breeze took us North past the Grenadines, St. Vincent and St. Lucia. We could not afford the time to stop at every island so we studied the pilot to find the best anchorages for our size and draught. Martinique sounded inviting so we pulled in with the dawn on May 16th and woke a few lay-a-bed yachtsmen with our rattling anchor chain. Martinique proved to be exactly like a little bit of France - sophisticated jewellery and chic clothes set against narrow littered streets and smelly drains - flashy modern buildings alongside ornate historic edifices. In the park we found Empress Josephine, motionless and benevolent, gazing down from her pedestal at her descendants. She looked thoughtful, as well she might.

In order to see a bit of the island, we splashed out on the hire of a minibus and clattered our way to the coastal town of St. Pierre, where in 1902, the inhabitants had been boiled like jam by the guts of Mount Pelée. Only one man, a prisoner in a stone cell below ground level, had survived. The cathedral next door had been obliterated but its ruins give today's tourists some idea of its former glory. We felt compelled to call on the sleeping monster so turned inland and started climbing. We parked the minibus where it could look at the view and followed a path up into damp grey cloud. Every now and then the mist cleared and the sun spotlighted a section of coastline beneath us. Lucy, Joan and Iain were more interested in gathering pieces of pumice which they clutched to their chests and wedged in inadequate pockets. I think they had ideas of making their fortunes from the hard skin on the feet of their aged relatives!

As we headed back through the hills to Fort de France, we came across a line of parked cars. John pulled over and followed suit. We piled out and walked round the bend where we found the attraction was a wide waterfall which gushed over boulders to a tree lined rocky stream bed. It wasn't quite as pretty as one I know in North Wales but it had a certain charm.

Three figures flashed past me back to the minibus and emerged in the correct gear for the situation. While us oldies graced a comfortable boulder and dabbled our toes, superman and his two assistants commanded the heights, shrieked in the cold of the deep pool and dared each other to plunge through the curtain of water to a small cavity behind. Lucy recorded in her diary that Iain was the first person to do it but that she soon followed and Joan went in just as we were leaving because Pat said she couldn't come home unless she did. I know Pat would have said this only because she knew how desperately Joan wanted to keep up with the others. If she had left without trying, she would have been cross with herself and everybody else so Pat provided the spur. The crazy thing is that Joan is an excellent swimmer and not normally afraid of water but it wasn't the only time that we were to see her assertive nature undermined by a lack of self confidence.

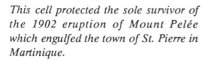

This cell protected the sole survivor of the 1902 eruption of Mount Pelée which engulfed the town of St. Pierre in Martinique.

We made one more stop, this time to look at a cemetery where the dead are provided with elaborate lodging in the form of marble chambers and bowers wrought with curly ironwork. Glazed panels revealed dusty coffins. Photographs of the deceased and his family stared out from wordy inscriptions, crosses, statuettes and a riot of flowers. I was intrigued by such gaudy tributes to the dead - far more spooky than the plain slabs of English graves in quiet greenery.

It was in Martinique that we met Charlie Marsden, a single hander in a little old gaffer called Rosemary. Style was synonymous with Charlie. He had that public school suavity and gangly grace that would probably ease him through most of life's difficulties. His rum punches were superb - the usual Caribbean mix of one of sour, two of sweet, three of strong and four of weak, but with the added touch of a sprinkling of nutmeg from Grenada. Andy and I felt we could have walked on the water between Rosemary and Christian Bugge that night! Charlie told us all kinds of stories and listened earnestly to ours. We chortled with him over his lack of funds and drank yet another rum punch. I wondered what he was seeking, for I assume all long distance single handers are trying to find something. We met Charlie again in the Azores in July. He had dressed Rosemary in signal flags from stem to stern in honour of Horta's annual regatta week. With any luck he made it back to that wife in Scotland, even if a few galley slaves fell prey to his charms on the way.

For two days we rejected the hustle and bustle of Fort de France in favour of Trois Ilets just across the bay where we could relax on the beach. Martin nobly attempted to teach the two giggly girls to windsurf and commented nostalgically that he had had a nice lady to teach him when he was in South Africa. It was a crowded anchorage so steering was important. Unfortunately, my planned moves on the board did not always work out as they were intended. I skimmed along trying to hold my stomach in if there were spectators around and as I approached a gleaming yacht I pulled the mast aft, ready to go about, stepped round it and straight into the water. This kind of thing only happened if there was a cockpit full of people or a dog who yapped incessantly so as to attract the attention of all the other yachts. I would then get tangled in the anchor line and the wind would either gust up or die away completely, making it extremely difficult to extricate myself from the situation. I did quite well when nobody was looking.

Time to move on again. We reported back to Fort de France to say an official 'au revoir' to the cheery customs officials. As we lumbered up the coast on a run, the wind curled round the boom and caught us aback. Since we had not fixed the usual vangs and preventers because we were anticipating a change of course, the mainsail hit the runner block and tore quite badly. Andy decided to take a reef in order to protect that part of the cloth until we could repair it in comfort at our next destination, the Leeward island of St. Kitts.

*   *   *   *   *

Passing close to Dominica and Guadeloupe, we arrived at the exposed anchorage of Basseterre on St. Kitts during the second night. In the light of day we left Christian Bugge rolling in a heavy swell for our first expedition ashore. We were struck by the neatness and orderliness of the streets. This quiet, easy going

Looking down from the upper section of the fort on Brimstone Hill in St. Kitts.

nation had recently gained independence and hoisted its own flag but it still had the stamp of British influence. The pavements were clean, the queues in the post office tidy and patient, the shops arranged with care. Immigration was a relaxed affair, not fast but reasonably efficient. Andy went to the cashier to pay his harbour fee of $7-50 (East Caribbean) and returned somewhat amused by his conversation with the girl there. In those few minutes he had discovered that she was wearing a shirt which had belonged to her deceased brother!

We did a circuit of the town which revealed exotic restaurants in old colonial splendour, beautiful batik souvenirs and a covered market where corpulent women with keen eyes were quick to spot newcomers. Joan was asked where she came from and the reply, "Jamaica" received such a look of disgust that we walked on quickly. Obviously Jamaica had a poor reputation in this part of the Caribbean. Pat bought some brown fruits which were given the thumbs down by the crew and in her diary Lucy recorded that it was a waste to pay a dollar for five sawdust fruits.

Taxis clustered in the wide circus around the town clock. Ever hopeful, the drivers leapt in front of us offering tours of the island but Pat had done her stuff as usual and discovered that there was an adequate public bus service. The following day the eight of us set out for Brimstone Hill - 'Gibraltar of the West Indies' and the site of a British fort which had played a large part in the wars between France and England in the seventeenth and eighteenth centuries.

The bus dropped us at the foot of the hill and we climbed the steep winding road to the lower walls of the fort where a notice displayed admission charges. Five dollars per person was more than we had expected to pay so John and Andy volunteered to wait while the rest of us went on. A man in a little hut took our money and seemed amazed that we could not afford to pay for all of us. An hour later, while the six of us were still trying to digest the wealth of information provided in the museum section of the fort, we bumped into John and Andy. It seemed the old man's wife had returned to the hut and, on finding two dejected figures unable to afford the entrance fee, had urged her husband to let them go in free of charge. He agreed on condition that they did not sign the visitors' book.

Reunited, we spent hours on Brimstone Hill enjoying the feeling of being in command of the island and imagining how it would have felt to be besieged here by the French in 1782. Governor Sir Thomas Shirley had held out for over a month while Hood engaged the French Fleet in a ferocious sea battle in an effort to send reinforcements. What utter despair the besieged troops must have experienced when heavy cannon and mortars which had been landed for their defence, were captured by the French at the foot of Brimstone Hill. Now they were turned to concentrate their deadly power on a small section of these fortress walls. Capitulation was inevitable and Hood retired to join Rodney's fleet. A year later, the English got St. Kitts back through the Treaty of Versailles and the Fortress of Brimstone Hill, with the addition of an upper Citadel on the highest point, remained in active use until 1854 when the troops were evacuated to go to the Crimea. The French did have one more go at St. Kitts in 1805 when they arrived with a monster one hundred and twenty gun ship in their fleet of twelve Sail-of-the-Line. Everything except Brimstone Hill was soon theirs and the French held the Kittitians to ransom, demanding forty thousand pounds as an alternative to pillage. When they received eighteen thousand which was all that could be raised, they went to the sister island of Nevis and held the Nevisians up for four thousand pounds likewise.

Thus the English remained triumphant guardians of St. Kitts and its Sugar Industry, the first to arrive in 1623 and the last to leave in 1983. For two hundred years it had survived the bloody battles which reflected the squabbles between France and England, finally being rewarded with years of peace under the great British Empire. Now it has to find its own identity within the Caribbean - not an easy task. I noticed a prominent display of photographs depicting the visit of Queen Elizabeth, Prince Philip, Prince Charles and Princess Margaret who had given their full support to the restoration of this British Fort. I suppose it will help them get money from the tourists.

At last we made a move to leave Brimstone Hill, paused at the lower portal to look across to Eustatius and reached the bus stop in sultry heat. We stopped off on the return trip to look at the Batik Factory. This was in a beautiful old sugar cane estate house, nestling amongst a profusion of tropical trees and shrubs. Inside the house, the batik designs of hibiscus flowers, rich sunsets and ships reflected the colourful scenes outside. We watched the deft fingers of the local girls applying wax to fine cotton cloth and wished we could have some of the finished work. We lingered on the porch, drinking in the perfumed air, then strolled reluctantly away through the trees. The path bordered a sugar cane plantation so Lucy, Joan and Iain salvaged some unwanted off-cuts and gnawed their way back to Basseterre.

We were anxious to meet our St. Kitts contact, Desmond Fosbery, a consultant surgeon who had been in the Seychelles at the same time as us. In 1982 he set sail in his Tahitian Ketch 'Jaho' with a Seychellois lad as crew - destination, his home in St. Kitts. His main problem turned out to be the crew who suddenly let off steam one day by taking an axe to the cabin. Somehow Desmond coped with the situation and eventually reached home where he resumed his place once more as respected doctor in the community. Christian Bugge's comfortable hip bath had once been the cockpit on Jaho so we could not forget Desmond. Not that anyone could forget Desmond. His very tall lean figure, dressed in an outfit resembling yellow pyjamas was well known on Mahe. The pallid face fringed with long fair hair and beard, seemed glum even when he smiled. He was a Buddhist, or something like it anyway. He did not kill mosquitoes or cockroaches and he had a living-in 'guru' called Mary. On that day in St. Kitts when he brought Mary down to Christian Bugge, she clambered over the rail with just a little help and announced that she was thirty years older than he was - "old enough to be his mother" she said, roaring with laughter. She was an amazing character - hair scraped to the top of her head in a chignon, eyes encircled by thick black liner, wrists and neck jingling with bangles and beads. Gravely, she told us how ill she had been but, judging by the way she tucked into her fourth iced flapjack, she had come through the worst and was likely to enjoy life for a few more years yet. She talked of the days when she had played the piano at concert hall standard and of her mystic composition. When the flapjacks were all gone, Desmond wrote in the visitors' book - 'We watched the old Christian Bugge rise from the waves in Mahe harbour 1981 and now welcome you to St. Kitts - well done' He helped his guru into the dinghy where she sat straight backed, waving exultantly.

We were all set to leave St. Kitts one morning , when a grey shape appeared on the horizon. We didn't normally get excited about the Royal Navy but this particular frigate, Ariadne, struck a chord in our minds. There was an officer on board who had been told by Andy's brother Richard, to watch out for us, so we couldn't possibly leave without saying hello. Well, things did not work out quite the way we had hoped. I suppose we weren't really suitable company for an officer! After giving us thirty minutes of his time it was left to Grenville Webb, the 'Buffer', to entertain us in the Petty Officers' Mess. This he did in style. While the officers were entertaining the VIPs of St. Kitts on deck that evening, Buffer Webb welcomed us aboard Ariadne via a 'hook ladder' at an inconspicuous section of the ship. John, Pat, Martin, Andy and I were entertained in the mess with stories and good beer. Every now and then a tray of leftovers from the other end of the ship would appear. "Anyone for pink lint?" shouted a sailor above the hubbub. This was a tray of luncheon meat. "What about some horse's neck?" A bucket of ready mixed brandy and ginger materialised in front of us. Buffer Webb was the most friendly and helpful person we could hope to meet. Next day he showed the children over the ship, bought them bars of chocolate and honoured Christian Bugge with a visit. He helped us top up with water and gave us some odd lengths of rope for baggywrinkle. We weren't sorry to have prolonged our stay in St. Kitts.

With time pressing, we decided we could only spare a few hours for Nevis. We anchored off Charlestown and went ashore to deserted streets. As we neared the first church, the joyful chanting and tapping of tambourines reminded us that it was Sunday. The whole population was in church for three hours. Even the bars were empty. We looked around, found a tourist place for a drink, snack and a swim, then set sail for Jamaica.

"I May Need Some Assistance"

"Should we carry a gun?" was a question we had to put to each other before we left Seychelles. The joint decision "No" was made, not because we disregarded piracy but because none of us felt able to cope with a shoot-out. If we were to be the target of a planned attack by hardened criminals then it was unlikely that we could match their weapons. Cunning and speed were our only hope. Now, as we sped towards Jamaica with a constant East wind on our tail, I began to worry just a little. In recent years there had been horrific stories of piracy where families had been gunned down, tossed overboard and their boats used to transport illegal drugs from the West Indies to the USA. The authorities had tightened up security and the drug traffic had spread to bigger ships so that small time piracy was less common. Still, my imagination conjured up lurid pictures of Christian Bugge and crew under savage attack. I broached the subject with the others one meal time because I felt we should have some kind of defence plan ready - just in case. At first they laughed at me. I thought of Lucy aged eleven and Joan aged nine, still with that blind faith in the actions of their parents. "Can't we at least talk about what we should do if anyone tried to board us?" I pleaded. Gradually, we constructed some possible scenarios and noted one or two ways in which we could strengthen moral if not our defence. Andy stressed that we should keep a very careful watch for approaching vessels, particularly at night. If we saw anything suspicious, we were to call everybody on deck for a show of muscle. If the danger proved real, either Andy, John or Martin were to get to the radio to send out a Mayday call. A heavy metal bar was strategically placed in the locker next to the steering wheel. What more could we do? At least I felt better for having talked it through.

Jamaica itself did not frighten me. When I lived there for two years at the beginning of the Seventies, it had seemed the only place in the world that was really alive. The violence was present but I had never felt personally threatened by it. There was aggression and stubborn pride but I had also found warmth and laughter. Would the extrovert Jamaicans have changed, I wondered. Would the economic and social depression of the intervening years have dulled their 'joie de vivre'? I was excited and nervous. Joan was also nervous. For her it was a big moment in her life to be revisiting her homeland but she was not over the moon about it. How could she be. Martin asked her if she was looking forward to going to Jamaica and I sensed a jumble of emotions as she gave a non-committal reply. She could not feel Jamaican. She had been born there but she did not begin to live in the true sense of the word until Pat and John came to her rescue at the orphanage. They loved her with protective British love, gave her a British passport, British accent and British values. No wonder she was uncertain of herself. Somewhere on that island was her real mother but she was nothing to Joan.

*   *   *   *   *

As the lights of Jamaica came up on June 2nd, six days out of Nevis, memories came tumbling out of the dark corners of my mind. Iain at one and a half years old had learnt his first words in Jamaica so it was not surprising that most of his early sentences had had 'man' tacked on the end. His white blond hair and dark eyes had charmed everyone. I remembered him singing 'Boom Shaka Laka', the latest Reggae hit, squashing his face into a large slice of water melon, growing plump and golden in the sun........Faces flickered by......eleven years was a long time. Kind Mrs Gayle, our Jamaican landlady for eighteen months, had died of cancer just before we left in 1973. A Yorkshireman of over eighty, our landlord for six months, was murdered in his Kingston home several years after we left. Gloria, my live-in maid, babysitter and friend for two years had kept in touch and I hoped to meet her again. Other Jamaican friends had become divorced and lost touch with us as they went their separate ways. Marriages in Jamaica seemed to slip and slide as if on marshy ground. The lucky ones found a way through and continued together on firmer paths but many lost their footing. The air had always seemed charged with excitement and temptation.

On Christian Bugge, John found that it wasn't only the air that was highly charged. Something he did or said, didn't do or didn't say (I am no longer sure which) ignited my temper and I threw a hot cup of tea over him. Fortunately, the splashes travelled far enough to cool down before reaching his bare back. I also cooled down and miserably tried to apologise, furious now at my own lack of self control and angry with Pat for laughing. I think this was probably my worst moment of the whole voyage, for I could cope with the moods of the rest of the crew and the underlying menace of situations which we were to encounter later but my own violence was another matter. John was incredibly forgiving.

*   *   *   *   *

We entered Kingston Harbour, guided by the lights as the last shadows of night were dispersed by the rising sun. There was not the slightest breath of wind now as we stopped at Port Royal for Customs and Immigration. As soon as we were allowed to take down our 'Q' flag to show that we had complied with health regulations, we headed on into the inner harbour. Our draught just made it over the bar at the entrance to the Royal Jamaica Yacht Club and by 8.00a.m. we were cooling off in the pool, determined to make the most of the one free day given to visiting yachts.

Next morning we motored further on into the harbour and anchored off Buccaneer Beach. Here the water was sheltered from the sea by Pallisadoes, a long spit of land which runs from East to West to form the outer defence of Kingston Harbour. It was a good anchorage, as close to the city as we were likely to get. What did it matter if the sand was coarse and grey or the sea the colour of Brown Windsor soup instead of Caribbean blue. We did not intend to relax.

We stayed for a week. The nights were airless but by 10.00a.m. every day, the surface of the water began to be ruffled and we had to row across to the beach (both outboard engines were irreparable) before the wind gained enough strength to make it very hard going. A half mile walk to the fast Pallisadoes road enabled us to catch a bus to the centre of Kingston, about nine miles away. This in itself was quite an experience. We copied the locals. Step into the road, out with the arm and a minibus would grind to a halt. However full it was, there was never any question of leaving prospective passengers behind. We were shoe-horned into seats or left to stand at crazy angles, sometimes almost sitting on another passenger's lap. In her diary Lucy recalls one particular journey.....'it was so crowded you couldn't move a single bit. I had to stand on one foot and put the other on top of it.' The drivers made a Grand Prix start from every bus stop as if their very lives depended upon it. In a way I suppose they did, for the whole bus service had been privatised. The faster a driver could deliver his passengers, the faster he could go back over his route and pick up more. He ran his bus into the ground with the minimum of maintenance until the suspension was shot, the seats worn down to the floor and the bodywork battle-scarred. Reggae music pumped its way round the bus to fuel the driver's skill and keep the passengers happy. The interior was usually clean and the conductor who sported a Rasta Tam or other flamboyant headgear, was always helpful. By the end of the week we were quite well known and even welcomed aboard with large cans of paraffin and bulging bags of fruit and vegetables.

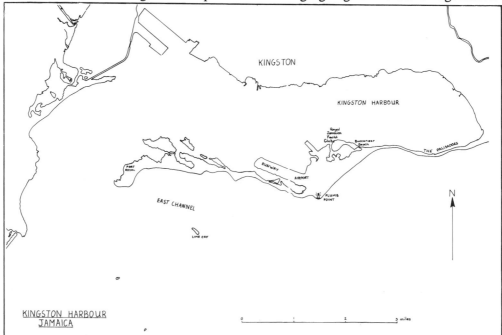

Down-town Kingston was a seething mass of gutter stalls and shop keepers who talked at the tops of their voices. The traffic rattled by inconsiderately. It did not willingly give way to pedestrians. We gripped each other so as not to become separated. We were offered coconuts to drink, peeled pineapples to suck, pretty slides to wear in our hair. For some reason Martin was singled out and a soft voice at his elbow offered him ganja. He declined. Andy and Lucy were confronted by a Jamaican man who beamed at them and said, "Dat ya daater man?" "Yes man" said Andy beaming back. The Jamaican nodded approvingly, "Fine daater man".

We passed on to the bank. It was crowded. Whilst Andy went upstairs to the Foreign Exchange Section, I became the target of a drunken old woman on the ground floor. She began haranguing me and the whole bank about something that was on her mind. Although I could not understand her broad patois, I realised it concerned my white skin. However, contrary to my first impression, she bore no ill will towards me but was simply holding me up as some kind of example. She tottered, swayed, shouted, and was finally persuaded to leave by a bank employee. I had been trying to sink through the floor but I need not have worried - nobody was really paying any attention and after a few more minutes I noticed other strange characters. The armed security guards lounged around unconcernedly.

On three of our trips to town we tucked into Jamaican patties at a stand-and-eat place called 'Mother's Patties'. Here we burnt our mouths on the most popular Jamaican take-away food - a spiced meat mixture inside flaky pastry. Iain had eaten his way through a few patties when he was only two years old so he was bound to be as enthusiastic as we were. Lucy found them too fiery and thereafter chose a cheese burger.

I loved the bustling down-town streets. Men strutted along the pavements with a greeting or good humoured insult on their lips. We always reckoned that if you looked them in the eye and gave as good as you got, then you were an accepted 'whitey'. The women walked proudly and often sensuously, dressed tidily in bright clothes, their hair mostly long but tied up, pinned back or plaited elaborately. Hair is something they feel strongly about. They spend hours shining and smoothing it with all kinds of preparations such as coconut oil and cocoa butter. Even a short 'Afro' style needs constant attention to keep the strands separate and glossy. Most school girls have long hair bunched in some way or plaited with ribbons, clips and slides. Joan was reduced to tears one day when two women scolded her in the middle of the street for having untidy hair. She was actually trying to grow it long enough to tie back but it was at that difficult in-between stage and none of the Christian Bugge crew were very clever with hair that reacted like wire wool. We liked Joan with short hair but she wouldn't let us use the scissors. After the incident in the street, Pat and John were visited by some old friends. While the adults chatted on deck, the thirteen year old daughter, Dawn, set to work on Joan for a transformation. It was a long, long process. The hair was brushed out in sections and smoothed with Vaseline until it was more manageable. Dawn put in twists all over, then replaced them with tiny plaits which hugged the head - a most complicated procedure. She made a geometric pattern with the even rows of plaiting and called it a corn row style. It changed Joan completely. Pat and John didn't

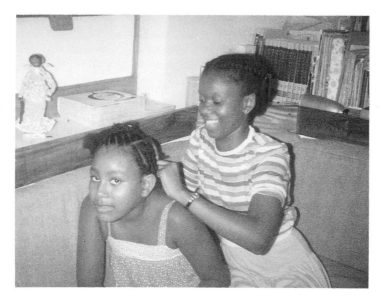

The new Joan.

like it very much but Joan was happy. I think she felt more Jamaican. Dawn told us that some girls wash their hair with the style in place and that it is only after one or two weeks that it needs redoing when the ends begin to work themselves out and look fuzzy. Needless to say, none of us were capable of reproducing anything like Dawn's handiwork.

Christian Bugge bobbed at anchor, alone, elegant as ever against a backdrop of misty blue mountains rising behind Kingston. For the first time since Seychelles, we put up the awning to keep the blistering sun off the deck. Sometimes we joined the locals under the beach showers and then returned to Christian Bugge to fight over the hammock.

One evening we were treated to a full Jamaican meal on deck by a French friend of ours. Andy and I had traced Gilou through the Alliance Français where she happened to be working in the Commercial Section. Neither of us had been good letter writers so there had been little contact during the previous eleven years. She was stunned to hear my voice on the telephone. We sat and gazed at each other in the luxurious bar of the Pegasus Hotel and tried to fill in some gaps. She was no longer married. She had been living with a Jamaican who had just gone to the States. She seemed more sophisticated than I remembered her - just as forthright but with a melancholy air. We each claimed neither of us had changed and after a few minutes I began to believe it. She took the four of us on a drive past the house where we had lived in Forest Hills, on up to Red Hills where she had lived with David, her husband. We stopped at a viewing point and looked down at the panorama we had known so well. For a few moments we shook off the years and remembered how we had explored this country together, delighting over the good and commiserating over the bad. Now Gil was a French Jamaican, more at home here than anywhere.

She planned a tremendous meal for the Christian Bugge crew - salt fish and ackee, chicken, rice and peas, johnny cakes and jerk pork. For those who are unfamiliar with ackees, they grow on trees in bright red pods. The pale yellow ackees inside constitute a national delicacy when fried with salt fish and seasonings. No other country is brave enough to eat them for they are poisonous if picked too early before the pod has burst open of its own accord. Each year there are recorded deaths from ackee poisoning but the Jamaicans consider it worth the risk. 'Rice and peas' is another national dish. The peas are what we would call red beans and they are cooked with the rice in coconut milk to make a delicious accompaniment to meat or fish. 'Jerk pork' is the belly part of the pig, highly seasoned with chillies and other spices, laid between allspice logs and cooked over a slow smoky fire in a pit. It used to be done in the country amongst the trees but Gil bought hers from one of the jerk pork shops which has sprung up in the city. Johnny cakes are crisp-fried risen dumplings, very good with salt fish and ackee. We could hardly move after this feast. Gil bedded down in the saloon and left us next morning after a leisurely breakfast. She and I vowed to keep in touch!

To find Gloria who had worked for us from 1971 - 1973, we walked down shabby back-streets in a poor area of Kingston. The chickens, pigs, goats and dogs which roamed the district did not attract as much attention as four white people on foot! Children looked up from their play on home-made go-carts. Men in long trousers and tidy shirts turned to stare at Andy's shorts and sloppy T-shirt. We came out onto a busy road and found the number we were looking for. As we went in through the gate, a girl directed us past the house to a line of outhouses in a dusty yard at the back of the property.

Gloria came out self consciously at first, plumper than I remembered her - coloured rollers in her hair. The wide smile turned to a laugh as she looked up at Iain who had once looked up at her and called her 'Goria'. She hugged us all and led us into her home. She lived in two tiny rooms with her third child, Melissa, aged three and an older daughter aged seventeen who had just had a baby of her own. Gloria's eyes apologised for the place but she busied herself with sending a small boy for soft drinks and ice. Then she pulled out some glasses and a bottle of fortified wine for a celebration. We felt uncomfortably large in the room which had only enough space for a table, two chairs and a dresser unit. The other room was completely filled by a double bed and a dressing table. There was no running water. Cooking facilities were in a communal kitchen across the yard. Lucy made friends with Melissa who giggled mischievously, while Gloria showed us her photograph album containing pictures which I had sent over the years. We talked about old times and our respective families. I couldn't help wishing she could have something better from life. She certainly deserved it. She was a cashier at a large downtown supermarket and yet she earned only seventy Jamaican dollars (about fourteen pounds) per week.

As the Kingston rush hour approached, we prepared to leave, anxious to get back to Christian Bugge before nightfall. Gloria was not happy about us leaving at dusk and told us many times not to get out our money in the street for fear of it being snatched. "Always have your busfare ready in your hand - nothing more" she cautioned sternly. Just as we reached the gate, her 'friend' appeared in his car and was pounced upon by Gloria who persuaded him to give us a lift to Buccaneer

Beach. He spoke little on the way. Perhaps he disapproved of our association with Gloria. We were very glad of the lift and paid him for the petrol.

We saw Gloria twice after that, once in her supermarket where she looked smart and efficient as she checked our shopping at the till and once when the security guard from the supermarket gave her a lift down to the boat for the evening. Although she had seen violent, poverty stricken times in Jamaica, she had not lost her zest for living.

My own zest for living was strengthened the day Pat, Joan, Lucy and I found ourselves facing the barrel of a semi-automatic weapon and the cold penetrating eyes of a very young policeman. We stood like wax models on the roadside while a second policeman searched the flashy car of the black Jamaican who had offered us a lift to town. A bus passed by and Pat and I exchanged glances - so much for speed. At least buses only crashed, broke down or caught fire (we had seen examples of all three). Our car driver had scorched the tarmac quite blatantly and seemed not the least bit surprised or perturbed when the flashing light and siren came up behind him. Now we stood waiting while the older policeman questioned the driver endlessly and made the search last as long as possible. At last he told us we were free to go. The barrel of the gun was lowered and the robot policeman moved away without ever having spoken. Mechanically, we got into the car. We felt duty bound to continue with our chauffeur because we were being watched and anyway there was no bus stop nearby. Our destination was a school where Pat had taught in the seventies and where Joan and Lucy were invited to join the Brownie Pack for the afternoon. We were late but glad to arrive at all. Lucy and Joan wore their bright orange uniforms from the Seychelles and told the Jamaican Brownies something of their round-the-world adventures.

We squeezed in two other expeditions during that week - one to Hope Gardens where we spent some time in the little zoo - the other to Spanish Town to the West of Kingston where we lingered in the Folk Museum. The zoo was more popular with the girls and the writing flowed in their diaries afterwards. Of the jaguar, Lucy wrote, 'He was very beautiful, I thought. He was also very thin but he had a beautiful head and a lovely sleek coat of yellow with beautiful dark spots. His paws looked so gentle and soft but I knew that they could easily rip me apart.' She felt sorry for the falcons who were in a small cage and commented, 'It would have been lovely watching them fly in the sky'. The lion cubs were understandably the favourites of both girls. Lucy was convinced that one of them smiled at her.

Our time was up and the awning came down but our plans for an early start on that Monday morning were to be thwarted by steering cable gremlins. Having taken on fuel and water at the Yacht Club, we cleared Customs at Port Royal and left the quayside to turn into the channel. As we began the turn, we lost our steerage but since the rudder position was gently rounding us up into the wind, Andy's rapid orders to man the anchor, averted disaster. Christian Bugge stayed put for the rest of the day while Andy, John and Martin fitted new cable on the starboard side. I knew we were very lucky that it had not broken just a little later when we might have been negotiating a bend in the channel with reef on either side.

Once more we said goodbye to Jamaica, this time in the dark, and we grouped on deck to identify the colour and flash interval of the lights which marked the dangerous shoals in the outer harbour. At 2055, with Plumb Point Light abeam, we knew we were clear of the cays and could steer along the South coast. Our route lay round the East end of Jamaica and up through the Windward Passage between Cuba and Haiti.

*   *   *   *   *

Three very ordinary days later, we were hugging the tip of Cuba, fighting wind and current to get far enough North to be able to bear away for the edge of the Great Bahama Bank and then Miami. We were motor sailing in a lumpy sea. Andy was on watch whilst the rest of us relaxed over a late lunch in the dinette. I was conscious of the proximity of the Cuban coast but not unduly worried for there was no sign of life, only wooded slopes and rocky shores. I had been baking bread that morning, hence the late lunch at 1400. It always took longer in rough conditions. In fact there was still one large loaf in the oven.

Suddenly, Andy put his head down through the hatch and said calmly, "I may need some assistance. There's a boat following us." Immediately my heart thumped and my face burned as I joined the stampede to get on deck. Martin was the only one who had not sensed the note of alarm in Andy's voice. He doggedly carried on eating.

We stared at the scruffy boat, wallowing in the choppy sea but gradually gaining on us. It had two short masts and an awning which partially hid a group of figures beneath it. Quickly Andy related how he had seen the vessel leave the coast a short time ago and set a course that was parallel to our own. He had only become anxious when it suddenly altered course and headed straight for Christian Bugge. "We must put up more sail" he said urgently. "We'll head out into the channel on a port tack."

Christian Bugge finds an extra turn of speed to escape gunfire off the coast of Cuba.

The US coastguard vessel Cape Upright takes a close look at us.

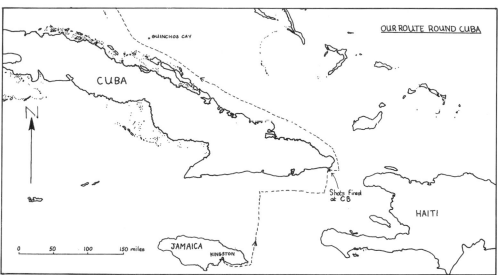

Iain, John and I moved towards the halyards. Pat started towards the saloon to keep the girls out of the way and to ask Martin to join us. The unexpected crackle of gunfire across the water stopped us in our tracks. For a moment I felt my legs would not take my weight. I was acutely aware of everything around me but I didn't seem to be in charge of my body. Cold fear took over. It was Andy who brought me back to life by urging us to continue putting up the sails. Meanwhile, he opened up the throttle. Then Martin appeared. Either he realised the urgency of the situation or he had finished his sandwich. He tried to make radio contact with an American base or any vessel in the area - silence. Halyards became twisted and sheets tangled as fingers turned into thumbs. Every time a shot was fired I ducked automatically and glanced at the others to make sure they were all right. Iain managed to look unconcerned and was working calmly and efficiently. Another round of shots........the old tub which pursued Christian Bugge was now within one hundred metres of her. At last we sorted the jumble of ropes. The staysail and jib filled with wind. Now that we were on a reach, heading away from land, we felt the old girl pick up speed and we began to pull away from our enemy. Our troubles were not yet over. Smoke began to issue from the engine room and to waft its way up through the saloon. Andy rushed below to find that the impeller on the water pump had disintegrated. He connected the bilge pump to provide a cooling system for the engine and we took turns at the handle, hardly daring to look astern. Joan and Lucy were shaking with fright as they clung to each other in the smoke filled saloon. Silently, we all willed Christian Bugge to go faster for there was suddenly nothing more we could do. My fingers began to unclench themselves as I realised that the intermittent gunfire had now ceased altogether. Moments later, our pursuers circled round and headed back to Cuba. We held our course towards Haiti and sighed with relief at being alive.

Now the questioning began. Had they intended to capture us, kill us or simply frighten us. Who were they? It seemed unlikely that the shadowy figures under the awning were acting in official capacity for the ramshackle boat flew no flag and made no attempt to communicate, except by bullets. On the other hand, if they had really wanted to board us, surely they had come close enough to fire with enough accuracy to force us to heave to. If we had not had the power to outstrip them - what then? We could only guess. When we reached Miami we heard stories of yachts being impounded and families held prisoner for many months, just for doing what we did - sailing too close to the Cuban coast!

I went below to put the kettle on and became aware of a hot bread smell. That large loaf had acquired a good crusty top but it was not burnt. The whole incident had lasted only thirty minutes or so - it was just that they were very long minutes!

Three days after the 'Cuban Crisis', Andy was again on watch while the rest of us were eating breakfast below. The call came for assistance and this time Martin led the way. We lined up along the deck, flexing our muscles and trying to look like twenty people instead of eight while a powerful speed boat travelled from the horizon to the hull of Christian Bugge in no time at all. There were two male figures aboard, one at the wheel and one on the bow. We stood motionless and tense. An American voice asked us if we knew where Guinchos Cay was. Andy's face showed surprise but he went below to the chartroom. The two men waited silently until he reappeared. "It's about fifty miles in that direction", Andy said, pointing. "OK. thanks" - they were gone amidst spray, back to the horizon.

It seemed odd to say the least - two men in an empty boat looking for an obscure cay in the Bahamas. They did not look like fishermen and they did not appear to be carrying diving equipment. Were they reconnoitring with something unlawful in mind or were we being unnecessarily suspicious?

The third time a meal was interrupted, occurred about forty miles off the coast of Florida when 'Cape Upright', an American coastguard vessel came to look us over. This time we lined the deck out of interest and waved cheerily. A team of men stood by the davits which held their inflatable dinghy but the skipper evidently decided we were not worth the trouble and dismissed them from their posts. Cape Upright left us in peace and we finished our supper.

Taurus

American Pie

.......Midnight, Fort Lauderdale.........Andy and I were beginning to think that Christian Bugge had turned into a pumpkin, for she was nowhere to be seen. We rowed round and round the anchorage at Las Olas bridge, peering at the dark shapes of boats which had been our neighbours for the last three days. In desperation we rowed towards the lights of the marina on the opposite side of the waterway. Maybe we would find Christian Bugge there, or at least a radio.

On the pontoon, the four of us separated. Iain and Lucy toured one side of the marina whilst Andy and I searched the other. Nothing. The smart yachts remained silent and unlit, offering no clues. We drifted back to the outer pontoon to debate our next move in a situation which seemed alternately grave and hysterically funny.

Five hours earlier, we had left Christian Bugge to be treated to a restaurant meal by a distant relative of Andy's sister-in-law. Jay Palliser and her son Deane had entertained us along with Deane's girlfriend Carole, teasingly nicknamed 'y'all' by Andy because of her Southern drawl. It had been the sort of evening to make the other Christian Bugge crew members drool - as much food as we could eat, with wine, coffee and liqueurs! After relaxing over more coffee in Jay's comfortable flat, we had returned to Las Olas bridge, drowsy from eating and drinking far more than usual and looking forward to crashing out in our bunks. Now here we were, wide awake, adrenalin pumping and no foreseeable prospect of sleep. I suddenly felt frustrated and irritable. The least John could have done was to leave a message in a bottle!

The purr of a small motor boat reached our ears and Andy hailed the approaching coastguard patrol vessel with waving arms. "Er....we've lost our boat. I wondered if you might have seen it" he called lamely. The two officials exchanged glances and looked us up and down. "How big?" one of them asked. Andy warmed up with a detailed description of Christian Bugge and told him that the co-owner was aboard. "Can you trust him?" queried the man. As it dawned on us what was going through his mind, we laughed. The idea that John would do a moonlit flit with Martin, Pat and Joan as crew, was somehow very amusing. As we chuckled, the other official scratched his head and said he recalled seeing a large yacht tied up at the Gulf Fuelling Jetty down-river. It sounded like a good lead so we thanked him and headed back across the water in the dory. As we approached the anchored yachts for the second time, a dog barked and a figure emerged from the cabin of Mayaroma. It seemed she had missed us the first time round but was now ready with a message. We climbed aboard, radioed Christian Bugge and by 2.00a.m. were home again, drinking Pat's coffee and listening to John's woeful tale.

It was really no surprise to learn that after we had left for our evening jaunt, the turning tide had become the cause of all the trouble. During our three days at the anchorage, we had discovered all its problems and acquired a reputation up and down the waterway. Our deep draught had forced us to stay on the edge of the channel which meant that the slightest change of position presented our stern or bow as an obstruction. We thought we had finally conquered this by putting out all our anchors - four in all - but on this particular occasion, the oozy mud and the six knot current which rushed out from under the bridge, were in collusion. Whilst the other yachts jiggled about as usual, Christian Bugge dragged her four anchors and slewed across the channel! The river police materialised within moments and issued an ultimatum......"Move or else...!", so John and Martin spent an interesting hour or two fishing for anchors while the evening rush of impress-the-girl-friend motor boats and drink-and-be-merry paddle steamers narrowly missed them in the fading light. With samples of intercoastal mud aboard and no place to go, they left a message with Mayaroma and cruised into the night, ending up at the fuelling jetty. Here they were not exactly made unwelcome but were warned that other boats would be out and about early on a Saturday morning so it would be best to

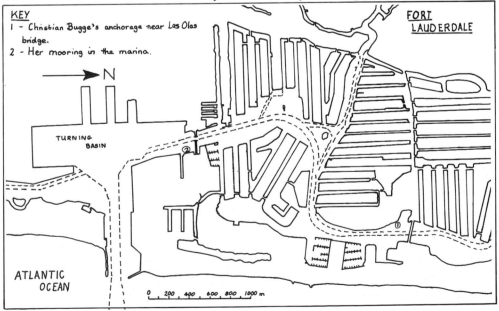

KEY
1 – Christian Bugge's anchorage near Las Olas bridge.
2 – Her mooring in the marina.

N

FORT LAUDERDALE

TURNING BASIN

ATLANTIC OCEAN

0 200 400 600 800 1000 m

move on by 6.00a.m. The lesson was beginning to strike home - on the intercoastal waterways of Florida, big is beautiful only if you have big money to go with it. We had resisted paying twenty five dollars a night to berth at a classy marina. With true British determination we had scoured every anchorage (grounding on several occasions) but now it seemed we had no alternative but to take advantage of our very understanding bank managers in order to stay in Florida long enough to do what we wanted.

We spent over two weeks on the outer pontoon of Marina Inn, close to the first bascule bridge at the North end of Port Everglades. Here the wash of waterway traffic jostled us in all directions until small sections of paintwork began to lose their grip in spite of heavy fendering against the piles. Christian Bugge had the look of a well travelled boat now. She rocked easily at her mooring and the crew moved in sympathy with her as they climbed over the bulwarks, tripped up and down the companionways, tenderly fingered the smooth wooden curves of the deckhouse. I was content that we had overcome so much and that we were almost on the last lap to Plymouth but I could not suppress a feeling of panic as I thought of having to part with Christian Bugge. I was well aware that it would have to happen. After all, with both families heavily in debt, how could we keep a ship like that in the manner to which she was accustomed? As it was, we were likely to have to rely on our long suffering relatives to help us through those first few weeks at home. How long would it take to think of dry land as home again, I wondered. Christian Bugge had taken so much and yet had given so much more. To me she wasn't just a yacht but a guide who held ghosts of the past and the key to adventure, through which the physical and emotional parts of me had come into sharp focus. Was I being too sentimental? Maybe. Even I had to admit that we could not live on sentiment for ever.

We entered into the devil-may-care spirit of Florida. We rushed here, there and everywhere on wheels, thanks to some good friends of Pat and John in Miami who were in the second hand car business. For the purpose of insurance, John went through the formality of buying an old Chevrolet on paper, with the knowledge that his friend would buy it back on paper when we left America. Since the amenities of Fort Lauderdale were decentralised, the car made all the difference

Approaching a bascule bridge on the intercoastal waterway.

Jay, Deane and y'all

in the world. For example, the main post office where poste restante mail was kept, was on its own miles from any shops. The yacht chandlery was in another direction, also isolated and the supermarkets were in shopping plazas geared only to motorists. Banks were scattered over the city but even these gave us problems. Having arranged for a further loan in the form of a draft, to be sent from our bank in U.K. to a bank near the marina, Andy was politely informed that they did not accept drafts for 'transients'! "Have a nice day" echoed after us as we wondered how we were going to be able to afford the day's supply of doughnuts, let alone the visit to Disneyworld. It took us ten days and several visits to six banks to find out that our money had been sent to a clearing house in Orlando and to make arrangements to collect it from the one bank which did not object to transients.

Meanwhile, Pat's sister Irene became our fairy godmother by offering Pat a loan. On this borrowed sum we drove to Irene's house in Fort Myers where we spent one night before carrying on up to Disneyworld. We felt very much like country cousins as we trooped into Irene's spacious home with grand rooms, plush furniture, indoor swimming pool, television in every room, not one computer but three, remote controlled garage doors and gadgets galore.

As we drove out of Fort Myers before dawn the next day, Pat joked about having married the wrong man. Enigmatic smile from John. "Just about every time I meet my sister, I have to borrow money off her", Pat went on teasingly. "She doesn't mind" retorted John. It was quite true. Irene was married to a doctor who was doing well for himself. She never had to worry about the cost of things and ate out whenever she felt like it, even for breakfast sometimes. It was hard for us to imagine that kind of life but it certainly impressed Joan, Lucy and Iain.

We arrived at the Magic Kingdom of Disneyworld just after opening time. Under starter's orders, we queued for our tickets which entitled us to any and as many rides as we could manage in one day. We shot away from the turnstiles onto the monorail, full of eagerness to cram as much as we could into the fifteen hours before closing time.

I loved it as much as the children did - the lavish spectacle of Disney scenes and characters - the dizzy rides. I squealed at hideous ghosts in the Haunted Mansion, shrieked as we raced through a waterfall on Thunder Mountain and stared wide eyed at the amazing working models in 'Pirates of the Caribbean' and 'It's a small small world'. I couldn't get over the slick organisation of the place. Large crowds were kept moving in a maze of hand rails which neatened the queue to a square and as we walked along the wide pathways between buildings, smartly dressed staff cleaned continuously with long handled brushes and dustpans. When we wanted to eat, we were processed in lines at Pecos Bill's place - hamburgers and chips with a paper cup full of crushed ice and a dash of cola. When we wanted a lavatory, the 'Rest Rooms' provided everything we could possibly want in a most hygienic and tasteful way.

I agreed with Iain that the most thrilling ride of the day was in Space Mountain. A roller coaster shot us into darkness dotted with twinkling stars and planets, then hurled us round impossible curves with no chance for our stomachs to anticipate what was coming. Joan stumbled into the open looking quite sick but she assured us it was great.

When the giant firework display spattered the sky at 10.00p.m., we began to yawn but forced ourselves to cover more ground, especially now that the crowds were dwindling. At 12.30a.m., staggering with fatigue, we fell into the car and headed for the Victorian Guest House nearby where we had booked a room for the night - yes, one room for the seven of us. We collapsed with laughter when we saw it - two frilly four poster beds and three mattresses on the floor in one long line. When the attentive landlord came up with extra soap and toilet rolls for the adjoining bathroom, we had difficulty in suppressing the giggles. It all seemed so incongruous somehow, almost as if we had become part of the Magic Kingdom which we had just left. Nobody could deny that it was a real bargain at at the agreed price of twenty seven dollars. The bed linen was clean and the shower worked. We slept like the proverbial logs.

Our second day in Disneyworld was spent at the Epcot Center, built only in 1982 with its entrance guarded by a colossal silver geosphere, entitled Spaceship Earth. Perhaps more appealing to older children and adults, Epcot presents modern technology with the usual fanciful approach. The past, present and future are linked under various broad topics and the rides attempt to be instructive as well as captivating. Spaceship Earth took us for a spiralling journey through the history of communications. World of Motion drove us through milestones in transportation history, while a slow ride through the Land Pavilion explored nature both in her wildest and her most cultivated states and showed experiments in future farming. For me the most sensational effect was in the Universe of Energy. We entered what appeared to be an ordinary theatre containing a large screen. In rows of comfortable seats, we watched a film on the development of fossil fuels and the energy forces of the future. Like everyone else I was totally unprepared for the next stage. The whole theatre moved forward through blackness into a prehistoric scene where the atmosphere was hot and steamy, where a wet earthy smell reached my nostrils. Pterodactyls swooped over us, a brontosaurus lumbered by and tyrannosaurus rex picked a fight with triceratops. It was unbelievably spectacular.

The children's favourite haunts were the Computer Halls and the Image Works where they could actually do something. They experimented endlessly with computer light pens and up to date games, stamped on brightly lit tiles to make music and walked through the swirling colours of the rainbow corridor. All this and much more was only half of Epcot. The other section was World Showcase where nine countries displayed their cultures in a variety of ways. In the U.K. pavilion, food and drink was available at the Rose and Crown pub and the entertainment was a bawdy street play for which all the actors and actresses were drawn from the audience. By the end of it, tears of laughter streamed down the faces of the audience (by no means all British) as the entire cast was persuaded to lie flat on the ground! This contrasted with the host country's entertainment which was a slushy presentation of the story of America. Moving models of Mark Twain and Ben Franklin were so incredibly life-like that I was taken in for a while but after the initial amazement at this special effect (audio-animatronics), I lost interest

A little bit of England in the World Showcase of Epcot.

The impressive Epcot geosphere.

and dozed in the extra wide, extra soft seat. Pat told me afterwards that John and Joan had both enjoyed a really good deep sleep there!

The climax of the day was yet another firework display, this time linked with stirring music and laser beams which criss-crossed the heavens. After that I felt so satiated with dazzling effects that I could take in little else. It was time to leave anyway.

With Pat in the front of the car, pinching herself and John to keep awake, we arrived back at Christian Bugge soon after 4.00a.m. and remained blotto in our bunks until midday. Not even the clanging bell to warn motorists that the bascule bridge was going up and the barrier coming down, could disturb our slumber.

* * * * *

It was the Christian Bugge Commando Unit which tackled the long term shopping in Fort Lauderdale. The group stormed the automatic doors of the supermarket and immediately spread out to take cover in the aisles, each person armed with his own personal list - his task to obtain the cheapest possible brand of each item. The leader of the unit took up a central position, easily accessible to the returning scouts. If they failed to find the correct item, they were immediately sent back into the fray to do better. Unsuspecting shoppers were suddenly faced with gaps on the shelves or were run down by the trolley of an inexperienced operator. The mission was successful. Christian Bugge was loaded with stores for up to two months. Provided we did not go astray in the Bermuda Triangle we would reach Plymouth reasonably well fed.

The three members of the Cadet Force mounted their own expedition to another supermarket where five dollars was offered for the return of one hundred shopping trolleys to a gated area where a ticket was issued for each one. Most shoppers could not be bothered to take their trolley back inside so the car park remained littered with them. The team set to work and had twenty tickets within the first few minutes. Then the pace slowed as they had to wait for more customers to exit. They even pushed full trolleys out to the owners' cars to be sure of getting the ticket and said politely, in their best English accents, "Can I take your trolley madam?" After a couple of hours they had gated two hundred trolleys and exchanged the tickets for vouchers to the value of ten dollars. Iain managed a further deal with a prospective customer who was willing to exchange cash for a five dollar voucher. It surprised me that at no time did I ever see American children getting in on the act. Were they all away at camp or was it simply that they can get that sort of money any time, without having to work for it?

I don't think it was pushing trolleys that aggravated Iain's ingrowing toe-nail but whatever it was, we were forced into taking the sore and suppurating appendage to a doctor. Once again the medical insurance turned up trumps and Iain came out of the surgery minus part of his toe-nail. He bore it with equanimity and did not let it prevent him from swimming in the Marina pool. It was sheer luxury to have a pool so close that we could go for a dip several times a day and more often than not, have it to ourselves. The two girls glowed with health and made fleeting friendships. I was pleased they were getting a real break before the last part of the voyage.

Saying goodbye to Fort Lauderdale was relatively easy but parting with our long standing crew member, Martin, was much harder. When he put it to us that he had been offered money to crew for a South African friend, we knew we had to let him go. Considerate as ever, Martin assured us that if we needed him for the last leg then he was quite prepared to stay. We couldn't be that cruel. After nine months of being dependent on our tenuous resources, it was no wonder that he was feeling restless. What a relief it would be to be able to walk into a bar with cash in his pocket, free of the Bugge strings.

He left several days before us, on a delivery job with his friend Leon. Like us they were heading for the Azores. Meanwhile, we stayed for the crazy Independence Day celebrations - the water seething with big boats and little boats charging out of the harbour entrance for a view of the beach firework displays. We stayed for a series of phonecalls to England, to see if either of Andy's brothers or any friends could take time off to join us for the trip to the Azores, or Azores to Plymouth. Needless to say, we could find nobody in that enviable position at such short notice. There was nothing for it but to set sail with seven.

Orion

Water and Wine

Standing bleary eyed at 0200, with my right arm aching from ten minutes at the hand pumps, I missed our departed eighth crew member. It was gradually becoming apparent that some planking had eased a little too much and was allowing a steady trickle of water into the bilges. I worried about it but was persuaded to keep my fears under control by Andy's lack of concern. He and John put their heads down into the cavernous spaces below the floor and began to suspect a small area at the forward end of the keel. "Nothing to worry about though" said Andy. "You should see the amount of pumping that some boats have to do."

Although the actual quantity of water was not great, we all agreed that the situation needed careful monitoring. During the early part of the voyage, thirty pumps every three hours had been sufficient to keep the forward bilge dry but now we were having to shoulder two to three hundred pumps over the same three hour period. "Have you pumped the bilges?" became the standard greeting at the change of watch because it was no joke having to do double duty at the handle. It was only when we got into the colder waters of the North Atlantic that we appreciated the job as a means of keeping warm! I should mention here that, once upon a time we did possess two electric bilge pumps which gave up before we ever left South Africa. Our arms could not afford to give up, especially now there were two less.

With only five of us capable of taking watches, we had to devise a new system. During the first day out of Fort Lauderdale, we settled on a fixed rota which excluded Iain from night watches because of the pressure of his school work. He was to take lunchtime and evening watches and Andy and John were to cover an extra watch each to allow Pat and I to cope with teaching and cooking. Thus the twenty four hour period was divided into two hour watches as follows:

Looking towards the shower cubicle in the main heads.

I made up this little jingle to help visiting landlubbers

RULES OF THE LOO

USERS OF THE LOO BE SEATED
TILL PERFORMANCE BE COMPLETED
        RISE UP CAREFULLY AND STAND
        GRASP THE HANDLE IN YOUR HAND

PUMP THE BOWL TILL IT BE FREE
COMMIT THE CONTENTS TO THE SEA
        THREE OR FOUR PUMPS SHOULD SUFFICE
        BUT NOW THERE'S MORE TO MAKE IT "NICE"

FLICK THE SWITCH AND KEEP ON GOING
EIGHT AT LEAST TO KEEP IT FLOWING
        THIS WILL BRING THE CLEAR FRESH WATER....
        AND IF YOU DON'T DO WHAT YOU OUGHT'ER

. . . .

YOU WILL FIND YOU'LL SEE ONCE MORE
WHAT YOU'VE DONE AND SEEN BEFORE !

0600 - 1000	Andy and Helen
1000 - 1200	John
1200 - 1400	Iain
1400 - 1600	Andy
1600 - 2000	John and Pat
2000 - 2200	Iain
2200 - 0200	Andy and Helen
0200 - 0600	John and Pat

During the four hour periods allotted to husband and wife as a team, there was room for flexibility. For example, I usually preferred to take over from Iain at 2200 but occasionally felt so tired that Andy stepped into the breach and woke me at midnight. The dozing partner always remained fully clothed on the saloon berth where he or she could be roused in an instant if necessary.

On the 0200 - 0600 watch, Pat and John took the responsibility for pumping the day's supply of fresh water from the main tanks to the five gallon header tank above the galley. It took a good ten minutes pumping before the sensor device triggered a red light to show that the tank was full. On long passages it was regular procedure to restrict ourselves to the five gallons of fresh water per day and to switch the electrical system over to sea water. The effort of trailing to the galley sink every time we wanted fresh water made us stop and think about what we were doing. Although the five gallons was readily available, we were again made aware of our action by the one and only tap which required considerable hand pressure to operate it, unlike the others which needed nothing more than the twist of a knob to produce an electrical contact to start the pump and make the water flow. Since the galley sink was supplied with both fresh and salt water, it was important to remember which tap was which. I recall only one major disaster - the day I made salt water tea. John's face was a picture.

To anyone who has never left the comfort of a piped water supply where you think nothing of letting the tap run while you clean your teeth or wash your hands, five gallons of water for seven or eight people must sound unbelievable but once into the routine we found it adequate for cooking and drinking purposes. Pat and I boiled vegetables, rice and pasta in a mixture of salt and fresh whilst the men washed the dishes in hot sea water but there was never any restriction on tea or coffee. On our longest passage from St. Helena to Trinidad we had made our two hundred and eighty gallon water supply last five weeks with one tank to spare. In port we normally needed to fill up after ten days!

The thinking behind the decision to store our water in numerous flexible tanks in the bilges was as follows:

1) Small tanks presented less of a sloshing problem when underway.

2) With each tank separated by valves, possible contamination or leakage would not be a catastrophe.

3) Flexible tanks could be moved easily if it was ever necessary to get to the bilge area in a hurry.

Although we never actually changed our minds on these major points, we felt the quality of our particular bags left a lot to be desired. When the tanks first arrived, the welded seams of three of the inner bags were faulty so we returned them to England for replacements. During the ten month voyage, two more began to leak water from the inner section to the heavy duty exterior. This time John repaired them with a hot iron and we had no further problems.

As we slipped easily into the new routine I wondered if Martin was glad to be back on a modern boat with lightweight gear or whether he would spare Christian Bugge a nostalgic thought now and then.

For four days we had little or no wind and the sun was our constant companion. The hours flowed into each other as the sparkling Gulf Stream pushed us Northwards. In that giant aquarium our trailing log tangled constantly with weed and a group of magnificent dorades stayed in the shadow of our hull, clearly visible through the turquoise water. We got to know each one so well by its size and colour that when the biggest and most beautiful fish finally hooked himself on our line, we mourned the destruction of such beauty even though we had no intention of missing the chance of fish for supper. Martin would have been ecstatic about such a catch. John groaned.

The weather was perfect for a lazy sail and although the winds were light, the Gulf Stream carried us at speed. In the Tropics Andy and I had often stripped off in the stern and thrown bucketfuls of sea water over each other. For a time it was warm enough to do this again. With washing up liquid or shampoo to work up a lather, we subjected our bodies to a salty scrub, followed by a salty rinse. (Pat and John were far more modest and always preferred the shower in the main heads for their ablutions) At the time we felt refreshed but the salt left an unpleasant tackiness that lingered. Still, it was better than nothing. Joan and Lucy usually waited for rain. As soon as it started, they would rush out on deck with towels and soap and take their shower under the main or mizzen boom where the water gushed from the sails in a steady stream. They would whiten themselves all over, shrieking and giggling if they thought anyone was looking at them.

The rest of us were not idle in a rainstorm. We secured buckets under the deckhouse drainage hole where rain collected quickly from the curved catchment area of the saloon roof. Normally, our dirty clothes were hidden away in plastic bags where they fermented until we arrived in port but a couple of bonus buckets of soft rain water meant clean knickers all round! Out with the soap powder.

On the fifth day out of Fort Lauderdale the South West wind began to pick up and at 0200, the most popular time for sail changes and disasters, we gybed carelessly and tore the mainsail. We stowed it on the boom, poled out the headsails and left John on watch. As if in protest, Christian Bugge rolled furiously in the gathering swell and I felt myself pressed into the sides of my bunk as the waves played with the unsteady ship. After breakfast, Andy patched the tear and, with the mainsail flying once more, the roll became slower and easier.

The wind stayed much the same for the next few days and, as we levelled with Cape Hateras on Latitude thirty degrees North, we began to turn a little more to the North East, away from the coast and away from the concentration of the Gulf Stream. The only weather forecasts which we could pick up on our radio, were from a Colorado Time Station which also gave out ocean storm warnings. It rattled off as much information as it could in the space of one minute before the next time signal. This proved invaluable to us in positioning the high pressure area centred on the Azores throughout the summer months. If we could pin-point it accurately, we could use it to bring us down on the Azores from our North Easterly course. Whatever happened, we did not want to find ourselves in the middle of that high, struggling in the Horse Latitudes.

On July 17th, nine days out of Fort Lauderdale, we crossed from one time zone to another and altered our watches to GMT plus three hours. Then, three good days of moderate South Westerlies were followed by three frustrating days when there was only the whisper of a wind from anywhere but the South West. Perhaps we had misunderstood those gabbled forecasts after all. We motor sailed for a while to charge the batteries and relieve the tedium at the same time. I even got carried away with my baker's duties and produced deep fried doughnuts for tea. That must have done the trick because the wind strengthened as we ate them and the following morning it growled Force six from the West South West. Angry waves and an ominous dark line across the sky caused someone to say, "This is more like the North Atlantic we were expecting". We removed the jib and took three reefs in the main just in time to absorb the shock of the expected rain squall. A torrent of water was emptied over us but the sky cleared quickly and the fresh wind rocketed us into the next time zone - GMT plus two hours.

There were no more rain squalls. The nights were clear enough for Polaris sights and the days full of Northern sunshine with the suspicion of a chill in the air. I drank in every delicious moment on deck as if it were my last, enjoying the long rolling seascape. We were averaging between one hundred and twenty and one hundred and forty miles per day and our compass course varied little from one hundred and ten. As we came within five hundred miles of the Azores, the wind gradually veered to the West and we passed into the next time zone - GMT plus one hour. Somehow it made us feel very close to home.

Our approach for Faial was perfect. We passed between Corvo and Flores, the Northernmost islands of the group and our spirits were so high that, when the wind threatened to die away, Andy, John and Iain hurried to raise the topsail for a triumphant finish. They didn't even object when the wind veered North West and they had to gybe ship, topsail n' all, at that unsociable hour of 0200.

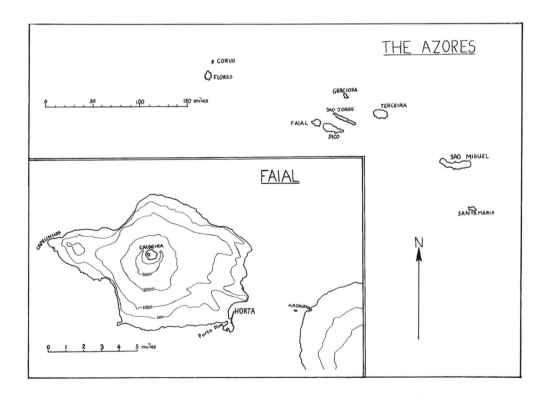

Three people were needed to manage the topsail yard.

Faial came up with the dawn, veiled in cloud on the blushing skyline. Iain was more awake than usual and climbed the mast just to make sure the island was really there. We sailed close to the coast, past the dusty barren Western tip known as Ponta dos Capelhinos and as we came round the South end of the island in a light North Easterly, we decided it was time to switch on the iron topsail if we were to make Horta by tea time.

The coastline became greener as we neared the bay of Horta, protected to the South by a narrow necked peninsula of ancient volcanic origin and overlooked by the conical outline of Pico island, four miles away. Down came all our sails in good time for the approach to the harbour entrance and we congratulated ourselves on our twenty five day passage from Fort Lauderdale. Behind the harbour wall we felt the heat of the afternoon sun and the festive atmosphere of the little town. People strolled the quayside to smile at new arrivals and there was a gentle hum of activity on and around the calm water. A strong smell of fish wafted over us from the cluttered work boats ahead. As we stood with coiled warps at the ready and eased Christian Bugge into the side, the wall beyond came into focus. It was crammed with brightly coloured murals stretching way along the quay. My immediate impression was of hundreds of yachts, some flat and crude, others ploughing along realistically in a blue sea. There were animals, stars and cartoon figures symbolising the names of yachts, whilst distant places and long forgotten dates stood out in bold paintwork. Palm trees, setting suns, giant insects, fish, flags and flowers all appeared as decoration in this gigantic piece of folk art. John turned to me and grinned. "Better start planning the Bugge patch", he said as he stepped ashore to make the bowline fast.

After straightforward Customs formalities, we received our first visitors - Martin and Leon. They had arrived several days before us and talked animatedly of a stormy passage from Fort Lauderdale and three days on the beautiful island of Flores. It seemed that we had been lucky enough to encounter only one brief squall. As for Flores - well, we would have liked to explore the other islands in the archipelago but we just did not have the time. We were aiming to reach Plymouth before the end of August and that meant we could allow ourselves only a few days in port.

Martin told us about the Public Bath House just along the quay and, knowing that we had no Portuguese currency as yet, he pressed some change into our hands so that we could go for the long awaited fresh water wash. Gathering towels, soap and clean clothes, we hurried along the quay. For twenty five escudos each, Pat, Joan Lucy and I were shown into the ladies' shower room of the Balneario Publico. There were only two showers. Since we all needed to shampoo our hair, time passed quickly as we took turns in the cubicles. Just as I was emerging from behind the curtain, starkers and dripping, the lady in charge pushed the door wide open and directed a stern speech in my direction. I do not know a word of Portuguese but from the way she pointed to the door and then to her watch, it was fairly obvious that we had outstayed our welcome. I wondered for a moment if I was expected to walk straight out or if I would be allowed time to put on my clothes but at last she retreated. Pat had a good laugh. After that we took more notice of closing times!

Our resolution to stay in the Azores for only a few days was swept aside when we discovered that Horta's big event of the year, 'Sea Week', was due to start on Sunday, three days after our arrival. We wandered with the crowds in the evenings, watched coloured lights and decorations appear in the trees, surveyed the bandstands and open air restaurants that were taking shape. The whole town was in holiday mood. Outside the Cafe Sport there was always a straggle of happy drinkers and across the road on the wall overlooking the harbour, lounged those who seemed to have all the time in the world to flirt, gossip or simply watch the rest go by. It was a time and place for relaxation and we felt compelled to stay with it, justifying our decision with the observation that we had arrived a little sooner than expected.

We explored the narrow streets and poky shops of Horta. Many of the terraced houses were small and plain but the seventeenth century churches were lofty buildings containing ornate treasures. Religion is of supreme importance to the people of the Azores. Even Sea Week could not start without the traditional mass and procession of fishermen. In the church, high above Porto Pim, they gathered with their families for the mass and then slowly made their way down the hairpin road and along the beach - a weaving line of men and women carrying religious symbols. Murmured chants lingered in the still evening air.

Although it is not necessary to be religious to attend Peter's place, the Cafe Sport has become a kind of sacred meeting house for visiting yachtspeople. Peter is everybody's friend and advisor. He can change your money, serve you with a coffee or a beer, tell you about the days when Faial was an important link in the Atlantic for submarine cables, or find you a doctor. It was Peter who told us where to go for a sail repair. Our staysail was past its best and needed a professional patch along its foot where the cloth was weakest. It was Peter who recommended the hospital for Iain's toe which had become infected again in spite of the American treatment. This time he had to suffer the removal of the whole toe-nail.

Martin was often to be found in Peter's bar and I believe it was there that he met Tristan Jones, the eccentric sailor and writer. Tristan was looking for a second crew member to sail with him to California via England, the Black Sea and the Indian Ocean, in a trimaran called Outward Leg. I assume that the name bore testimony to Tristan's own brand of humour since he himself possessed only one eye and one leg! Having decided that trimarans suited his onesidedness because they don't lean over like a monohull, he had agreed to sail this one round the world to demonstrate its particular safety features for the designer. On the other side of the coin, Tristan was being given a scenario for a new book and the chance to remain the nomad that he had always been. When Martin broached the subject of sailing with Tristan, Leon readily consented to let him go. We wished him luck and said goodbye yet again as he prepared to begin a new chapter of his life on Outward Leg.

In order to see more of Faial, we squeezed seven into a hired Fiat meant for four. Away from Horta, the hedgerows were blue with hydrangeas, a criss-crossing mass of blooms as far as the eye could see. When we stopped to alleviate suffocation and cramp, we filled our hair with flowers and picked fresh mint in the grassy verges. In the middle of the island, we walked up to the rim of the extinct Caldeira cone and looked down at the massive crater, two kilometres in diameter and four hundred metres deep. Here the vegetation was luxuriant but as we drove West we traversed a very different landscape where green slopes had been devastated by a mantle of lava and ash in the Capelhinos eruptions of 1957 and 1958. These had begun in the sea with jets of steam and gases. Then ash and pumice had been thrown up to form a new islet joined to the mainland by an isthmus. Onshore winds had sent ash to ruin the crops and force the nearby inhabitants to evacuate their homes. The later eruptions which had continued from May until October of 1958 had become a magnificent spectacle at night as fragments of incandescent lava were hurled more than five hundred metres into the air. Now the craggy wastes, shaded in black, brown and grey exuded an uncanny silence as if from another planet. Way above us on a serrated ridge, the heavy dust swirled at the touch of a breeze. As we drove away, we noticed the ruined upper floor of a stone built house, perched at a crazy angle on the barren slope. The bottom floor had been claimed by the lava stream.

Back in Horta after our sightseeing trip around the island, we relinquished the Fiat for feet once more and spent several hours appreciating the many exhibitions presented during Sea Week. I was struck by the obvious dedication of the people of the Azores to their local crafts and traditions. Examples of lace making, embroidery, cedar wood carvings, wicker work, whale bone models, pottery and weaving were all on display and in many cases, the craftsmen and women were there to demonstrate their art. The more unusual crafts attracted my attention. One lady was making the most delicate ear rings and brooches from tiny white flakes and silver wire. I was too dense at first to realise that she was using fish

Our ship looks travel stained at Horta quayside.

scales. She spoke English well, explaining her work slowly and carefully. I bought three items for next to nothing.

The fig tree pith work was more expensive, but again, probably not realistically priced, considering the labour involved. The girls were taking small sections of twigs from the fig tree and popping the pure white pith from the middle. These little cigarette sized pieces were finely carved by the more experienced women into delicate flowers and figures. In the fig tree pith museum we saw incredible composite scenes of houses, churches and windmills. The rigging on a sailing clipper was so white and fine that it was difficult to believe it was a carved substance.. The thought of such patience in this fast age was mind boggling.

John had been looking at scrimshaw work - drawings etched into slices of whale tooth. Armed with photos of Christian Bugge, he ordered two pieces for himself and two for us with the idea that we could use them for pendants, brooches or inlays for paperweights. When he went to collect them from Othon, scrimshaw expert, he was not allowed to pay. Othon had regarded it as a privilege to do such an interesting ship as Christian Bugge. As if that were not astonishing enough, he presented Lucy and Joan with navy blue sweat-shirts advertising Othon the Scrimshander.

This kindness was typical of the people we met on Faial and it made us want to revisit the Azores to discover the delights of the other islands. Of Sao Jorge, the island to the North, we learnt only that it produced excellent cheese. Having sampled it, we bought a large wedge for the last part of our voyage. Pico, which dominates the view from Horta, is so named for the impressive mountain which emerges from it (pico means peak in Portuguese). The guide book boasts of the island's fruit trees and vineyards but fails to mention the whaling station which still exists there and from which the whale is still hunted with harpoons in open boats. They catch less than one per week so I am told but I suppose it's not the kind of operation to attract tourists in the present climate of conservation, even if the tourists are pleased enough to buy the whale bone and scrimshaw work when they get there!

Corvo, Flores, Graciosa, Terceira, Sao Miguel make up the rest of this Atlantic archipelago which was formed by volcanic eruption in ancient times and colonised by Flemish and Portuguese settlers in the fifteenth Century. Each island has something special to offer but they all enjoy a gentle sub tropical climate due to the nearness of the Gulf Stream. In winter the temperature rarely drops below sixty degrees Fahrenheit and the average summer temperature is seventy four - perfect as far as I am concerned.

Having made the decision to stay for the whole of Sea Week we were determined to enjoy the festivities to the full. We persuaded a reluctant Iain to enter the open dinghy race which involved sailing to Pico and back, a total of nine miles. We pushed him off with a sun-hat on his head, and a packed lunch tied to the mast, then watched the red and white sail of the topper disappear in a conglomeration of dinghies and sail boards. After several gruelling hours of hot sun and light winds, we waved him home again from the harbour wall and gave him sustenance. He was really quite pleased with himself. "I made a windsurfer fall in the water", he boasted, "but it served him right for trying to cut me up. I was in the right." Eventually we found Iain's name on a list at the yacht club. He had finished third out of his class of five.

I did not have to persuade Iain to take part in the sand castle competition towards the end of the week. He walked with the girls to the black sand beach at Porto Pim on the South West side of the little peninsula which divided the town into two parts. In a roped off area the entrants were grouped according to age and told that they could build anything they liked. If it had been me I would have screamed my frustration and given up because the sand of Porto Pim was not the kind that modelled easily, even with the permitted buckets of water, but the children piled it up, dampened it, patted it, smoothed it, and managed to produce shapes that were vaguely recognisable. Iain, who stood at least a head taller than the slightly built Portuguese boys, hobbled around his patch with his foot in a plastic bag to protect his toe. He was going to a great deal of trouble to perfect the curve of two mounds of sand. I craned my neck to get an aerial view of this long, lumpy shape and suddenly it dawned on me what it was - a voluptuous woman lying flat on her back. I must admit she was clothed decently in a bikini but I guessed it would not be the judge's idea of first prize material. My eyes wandered to the next boy's model - an artistic sea lion - much more suitable.

Joan and Lucy were looking very smug all of a sudden. Already wearing T-shirts given away by the sponsors of the competition (incidentally they did not have one big enough for Iain) they were now handed ham rolls, cakes and fizzy drinks. The boxes of food came round so many times that they actually couldn't eat it all and had to pass some of it over the ropes to the four drooling parents.

The hydrangeas of Faial.

"Look at us!"

It was rare to find our saloon quite this tidy.

The girls cabin had lots of cupboard space for their bits and pieces.

Iain beamed as he gobbled ham rolls and guarded his woman from the careless feet of other competitors. The tension mounted as we awaited the judge's decision. No, no Hook or Smallwood had won the bicycle or the radio but we did not go away empty handed. Someone they pronounced as Jane Smallwood, won a novel in Portuguese for his sun-bathing sand woman. Lucy received a Portuguese story book for her model of Christian Bugge (minus sails) and Joan won the same for her rowing boat.

Dining out in the Azores proved to be something even we could pretend to afford once in eleven days. At the Capitolio Restaurant the seven of us enjoyed a good local meal for the equivalent of twelve pounds, and that included a carafe of red wine.

A whole case of red wine was one of the attractions in the Regatta do Canal, the offshore event for the big boats and the climax of Sea Week. The course lay between Faial and Pico, and providing there was enough wind, the race was to be two laps. To earn our wine, all we had to do was cross the finishing line within five hours of the start. This did not detract from our aim to win if at all possible and our other aim to show off Christian Bugge under full sail. The last was because we were conceited enough to think that our ship would add a touch of style to the spectacle.

Two days before the race, the organisers called a skippers' meeting and laid on a superb spread of food for them and their crews. Naturally the Christian Bugge contingent was there in force. We caught up on news of yachts we had met in the Caribbean and learnt something of other peoples' adventurous lives. The single handers fascinated me. There was Tom from 'Shuffle' who had been so nervous on his first lone voyage that he had not been able to sleep at all. A glutton for punishment, he was trying again after various disasters. There was Mike from 'Samphire', a slow spoken Cornishman with no history of sailing experience in the family. One day he had just decided to go and was not the least bit daunted by weeks alone at sea. These people set out with a small amount of knowledge and if they are not too unlucky, they survive and become proficient. Some are not so lucky. On the quayside was a small keel boat which harboured the macabre tale of its single handed skipper who had been found dead on board. He had drifted in the Horse Latitudes with no wind and had finally run out of food and water only sixty miles from the Azores.

We made a slow start in the Regatta, not surprisingly since we had taken on a crowd of Portuguese as extra crew. Most of them knew only a few words of English so spoken commands were of little use. After some untidy gybing and tacking, the lads caught on to what was needed, even though their previous experience was in small dinghies or on sail boards. Wind shifts and squalls kept us leaping about the deck all afternoon and although we knew we did not stand a chance against the lightweight cruisers in these conditions, we were enthusiastic to the end. In fact we didn't do too badly - not last anyway. The main thing was that both the British and the Portuguese got some fun out of it, that we got our wine and that we had looked good for the spectators.

The sand competition was held at Porto Pim where the sand was grey and coarse. Iain hobbled around with his foot in a polythene bag.

The spectators who gathered to witness my wall painting were far from complimentary. In fact their comments were extremely rude..............

I had gone to a great deal of trouble to select a spot which was both available and suitable for the Christian Bugge mural. Space was not easy to find. Some artists were having to paint over old patches which had become too indistinct to matter any more. Others resorted to autographing the pipes which ran along the top of the wall. I searched for a long time and finally selected a rough section of wall, low down at ground level. At least I didn't need a ladder. I painted a white background and left it to dry for twenty four hours before marking my design. Drawing the outline of Christian Bugge on such a rough surface was quite difficult but I managed to use the bulging part of the wall for the wind-filled sails and the smoother areas for the writing. I felt pleased with myself when it was finished and looked forward to painting in the colours the next day.

That next day began early with many loud mooings. As the noise worked its way into my consciousness, I remembered that Christian Bugge was definitely not moored in a field of cows, so what on earth was going on?

Up on deck the moos were deafening and as I looked towards the quay I was confronted by a long line of fidgeting rumps and steaming dollops which were quickly trampled under foot. The animals were tethered to a heavy wire cable which, presumably, was fixed to the wall for that very purpose. Some of the more stimulating murals generated a great bellowing from the critics as they nosed the wall and flicked their tails. I was anxious to know what they thought of my design so I vaulted ashore and walked further along. I might have known they wouldn't be ecstatic about it. Low murmured insults were being directed at my bit of wall and one beast had even managed to turn himself round to add his own decoration. I do think he should have had the courtesy to discuss the colour scheme with me before going ahead!

They stayed for most of the day until it was time to load them onto one of the inter-island boats. A team of men cleaned the quayside and I scrubbed the wall. The following day I completed the pictorial record of Christian Bugge's visit to Faial with the words SEYCHELLES TO PLYMOUTH - AUG '84

The noisy critics study the latest designs.

The finished mural reminds us that our adventure is almost over.

Plough

Topsail Finish

We left Faial at 2000 on August 13th. A featherweight North Easterly compelled us to motorsail Northwards for ten hours but then the wind began to pick up from the South East, enabling us to raise the number one jib and shut down the engine. The sailing from then on was a mixed bag as we skirted the high which was lying between the Azores and Southern England. During those next ten days the wind circled the clock and gave us a taste of tacking, reaching and running in turn. Twice we mended sails and twice we changed down to number two jib to ease the strain on the bowsprit while close hauling. When the wind steadied at Force four to five from the South, we achieved a record one hundred and sixty eight miles in one day but when it swung back to the East and died, our excellent average was threatened by a meagre total of sixty four miles from noon to noon.

No longer did I look forward to going on deck because the sky was often lowered by dull cloud and the air damp with misty drizzle. In spite of this there were only two days when we could not take the meridian sunsight, for our Guardian Angel usually made a hole in the cloud for us to glimpse the yellow orb at the appropriate moment. In the scudding shades of blackening night the pole star still managed to twinkle its companionship.

Whales, dolphins and on one occasion, a small hawksbill turtle, all popped their heads up to acknowledge Christian Bugge but after keeping pace with her for some moments, they moved away to a more pressing engagement.

The crew was particularly quiet, subdued perhaps by the nearness of England and the end of an adventure which had begun with the purchase of a decaying Redningskoite more than three years ago.

At night I snuggled deep into my sleeping bag to reflect on the voyage. With eyes closed, I listened to the familiar creaks and felt the motion of the ship so deep in my bones that my body spiralled weightless in my mind, as if in space. Two families had used all their resources to restore an old ship to life. Now they had to find someone else to care for her and make a new life for themselves. Three years ago, Christian Bugge had been thought of as a means to an end but to me now, her

future was perhaps more important to me than my own. Long before we were even born she had proved herself a tribute to Colin Archer's ideals of seaworthiness but we had helped her prove them again to a new generation, if they would listen. Our voyage had been a marvellous experience which we would never regret and never forget, but as it drew to a close I hoped that Norwegians would be interested to know that Christian Bugge was riding the waves again. Above all I hoped that someone would be able to afford to keep her alive and useful.

School went ahead with a kind of fury, as if everyone was trying to keep their minds off something. Now and then Lucy was able to contain herself no longer and jumped up and down shrieking, "I can't wait to get to England!" or something similar.

Joan's birthday provided a break in the routine. She and Lucy made Krazy Kake and flapjacks while Pat made the usual popcorn and Joan's favourite supper - spaghetti bolognaise. Lucy prepared a treasure trail of presents and we all played 'Up Jenkins' and the traditional 'Pass the Parcel' which was won by Iain. The prize was a plastic mermaid which swam with twirling arms when you turned a knob on her stomach!

On August 21st we calculated that there were only two hundred and ninety six miles to go to Plymouth and the girls began rehearsals for a 'Thinking of England' concert. They retreated to their cabins to practise recorder pieces, songs and poems in their spare time. They even persuaded Iain to recite the monologue, 'Albert and the Lion' without too much difficulty. At the performance two days later, Lucy's choice of poem, 'O England country of my heart's desire' received loud applause, although it did occur to me that this 'Land of thatched cottages and bees, And wayside inns where one may take one's ease' had little in common with the

England we were hearing about on the radio - a land of miners' strikes and inflation, drugs and discontent. I was beginning to realise that we had to face up to that England and help our children face up to that England. Though widely travelled, they had been cocooned from the cut and thrust of urban living. Now they had to meet the social pressures of a much larger peer group. Pop music, fashions, and electronic gadgetry would be thrown at them by the Media. Would they keep their heads and retain just enough of that worldliness acquired on the trip, to sustain their individuality? At the moment England was the elusive Nirvana. They were far more excited about it than if we had boarded a plane on Mahé and stepped off at Heathrow less than a day later! I knew how they felt. After all, they were going home, and everyone knows it's always more satisfying to arrive home after a struggle.

*　*　*　*　*

Friday August 24th - breakfast off Land's End.

Andy put through a radio telephone call to Robin who was staying with his other brother Richard in Plymouth. While the girls danced about the deck and I choked on my second cup of tea, in the chartroom Andy was holding a perfectly calm telephone conversation with Robin, as if he did this every day. Andy gave him our position and ETA which at that moment was dawn the following day. Robin confirmed that he would make certain telephone calls to begin the chain of communication designed to spread the word of Christian Bugge's homecoming to relatives and friends of both the Smallwoods and the Hooks. I could not bear to leave it at that. I put through a call to my father and heard his warm voice fill the chartroom as if he were on board with us. Lucy spoke to her Granny but was so overcome that she could say little more than hello.

Full of nervous energy, we raised the topsail to intimidate a French yacht on the same heading as us. Pat and the girls tidied the school cupboard to mark the end of the academic year and to pass the time. Now it was a question of waiting. We were anxious to fix our eyes on land but the shores of England lay hidden under a grey cloak of moist air. We cleared the Lizard and yet still saw nothing. Now, gliding swiftly in a flat sea, with a moderate North West wind on our port beam, it soon became obvious that our earlier ETA was wide of the mark. We called Robin again and told him to expect us before midnight.

Shivering in the chill night air, we stared at the fixed light across the bay and joined in with Andy as he sang, 'Me father was the keeper of the Eddystone Light - He slept with a mermaid one fine night'. More lights and shadowy land began to appear until at last we cleared Rame Head and entered the Sound. Meanwhile Robin was sailing out from Plymouth in his small mini-tonner. The two vessels exchanged searchlight beams just off the Breakwater and the elegant old lady followed her flighty young pilot to the Customs House Quay at Millbay.

Looking up from the bottom of the dank wall at low water, I saw a row of smiling faces and a welcome banner.

Our chartroom was spacious and convenient.

"...I saw a row of smiling faces and a welcome banner."

Happy homecomers - from the top, Lucy, Joan, Andy, John, Iain, Helen and Pat.

Glossary of Terms

Mizzen	- Small mast and sail at stern.
Gaff	- Spar at top of mainsail and mizzen.
Boom	- Spar at bottom of mainsail and mizzen.
Jib	- Sail at front of boat attached to end of bowsprit.
Staysail	- Sail behind jib attached to bow of boat.
Topsail	- Above mainsail at top of mast.
Runner	- Stay holding mainmast back to a chainplate.
Sheet	- Rope for adjusting angle of sails.

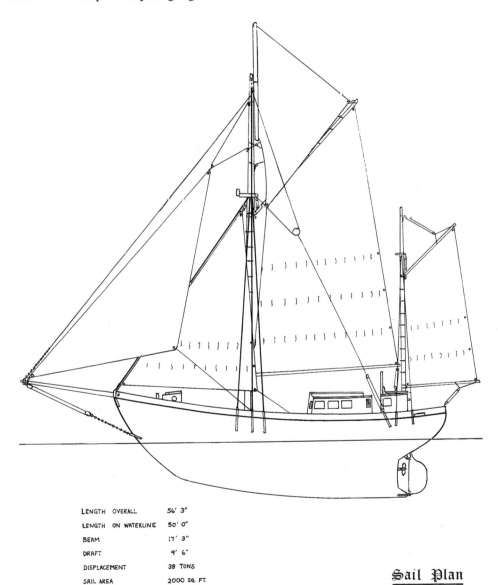

LENGTH OVERALL	56' 3"
LENGTH ON WATERLINE	50' 0"
BEAM	17' 3"
DRAFT	9' 6"
DISPLACEMENT	38 TONS
SAIL AREA	2000 SQ. FT.

Sail Plan
Christian Bugge

Afterword

Since the rebirth of Christian Bugge, many Scottish lads and lassies have enjoyed their first sailing experience aboard her. Lying at Kip Marina on the Clyde, she has taken groups of sponsored young people for sail training holidays under the auspices of 'Sail and Adventure Scotland'. She has also been the centre of a marina display at the Glasgow Garden Festival of 1988, attracting the admiring glances of visitors from all over the world.

Andy and Helen have not settled easily to a land based life in South Wales and talk of future adventures. On the other hand, Iain and Lucy have coped admirably with the pressures of a large comprehensive school. They have drawn on their trans-ocean experiences and appear to be growing up with a broad outlook on life.

John, Pat and Joan have been in exile in the Bahamas after finding no suitable jobs in the United Kingdom. They yearn for their home in North Wales.

Martin has had his own adventures with Tristan Jones, finally returning home only to make more plans for blue water sailing. He cannot subdue that restlessness which is in his bones.